FROM UNDER THE TRUCK

A Memoir

Josh Brolin

HARPER

An Imprint of HarperCollins*Publishers*

HarperCollins books may be purchased for educational, business, or sales promotional use. For information, please email the
Special Markets Department at SPsales@harpercollins.com.

FIRST EDITION

All photographs courtesy of the author.

Designed by Elina Cohen

Library of Congress Cataloging-in-Publication Data has been applied for.

ISBN 978-0-06-338218-3

24 25 26 27 28 LBC 5 4 3 2 1

For the Whole Brolin Clan

WHATEVER ELSE IS UNSURE IN THIS STINKING DUNGHILL OF A
WORLD A MOTHER'S LOVE IS NOT.

—*James Joyce,* A Portrait of the Artist as a Young Man

YOU CAN'T IGNORE THE ANIMALS IN YOUR BONES.

—*Glasgow street graffiti*

CONTENTS

FROM
UNDER
THE
TRUCK

IT CLAWS AT ME with its long, thin nails.

I wince as I hear my parents inside the house fighting, but with the whinnying of the horses so loud, I can't be sure it's them or the dogs or the wolves, whose cages I'll have to clean soon. Even with the sound of the leaves in the trees, the cold grass on my back, there's the strange feeling that all the oxygen in the world is drifting in a direction away from me. Rain is coming though. It isn't here yet, but I can feel it coming.

2023

LIFE WITH JANE WAS TUMULTUOUS, but I miss it.

I'm sitting in a broken-down café in the desert, writing. It's hot and uncomfortable. It happens to be the same desert I visited as a child with my mother, also hot and uncomfortable. I sat beside her, time and time again, baking under an unrelenting 115-degree sun. I knew how these things went with her: Lather with oil ("Get my back. More on my back!"), lay back on the plastic lounge chair next to the shuffleboard inlay, Dr Pepper in her right hand and a burning Kool King in her left hanging in zero-gravity anticipation. Now bake: a human brownie forgotten, compost in the wait. And her little blond eight-year-old kid who jumps adobe walls and looks for rattlesnakes on the outskirts of unused parking lots sits fidgeting, barely able to hold his budding hormones still enough to have half a conversation.

My childhood was on a leash of the whims of my mother. She drove sixty thousand miles a year because as a flight attendant in her early twenties she got bumped around one too many times and was afraid to fly unless she was drunk and it involved some mysterious adventure with sex and a few dinners, usually with the pilot. Otherwise, it was always the car: 1978 green Cadillac, mid-80s Grand Cherokee Wagoneer, and a timeless 450SEL Mercedes-Benz that she crashed at least seven times. Over the years, those are the three I remember barreling down all the highways in.

After I jumped back onto the adobe wall, burning myself on the dull shards of glass that were imbedded at the top for "added security," I would see her from high above, small and dark brown, with heat waves coming off her that would make the palm trees in the background undulate like looking into a pool after someone had just jumped in: the bullfrog-voiced cheap Texan who had finally made something of herself out here in California, my mother. She knew everyone and everyone knew her. She was that person who would talk to any Tom, Dick, or Harry at the bar, then be in the kitchen cooking with the chef by closing. Jane was infamous. I (and everyone else) was just along for the ride.

She picked up her Dr Pepper without opening her eyes, took a sip, and put it back down precisely on the same ringed spot it had just been pulled from. Next, the last drag of her menthol stick before she flicked it low and tripping into the pool.

"What are you doing?" she asked me.

"Nothing. I was just looking for rattlesnakes."

"They bite, you know."

"I know they do. I was careful and collected them by the tails. I put them all in the car."

"No, you didn't."

I walked toward our motel room to masturbate—push two pillows together: instant vagina.

"It's too hot out here," I said leaving.

"It's never too hot," she retorted.

I couldn't see when I walked into the room because the sun had been so bright it melted my corneas. I sat on the bed while the swamp cooler above me spit and clanked. Sweating, I grabbed the two pillows on the bed and stood up to go to the bathroom when I heard the door close. "Mom?" . . . then the sound of retching. "Are you okay?" More retching. "I have heat stroke!" More retching. "Can I go get somebody?" "No! I just have to wait it out.

You should lay out. You haven't gotten any sun." "You're throwing up because *you* laid out. Why the fuck would you want me to?" "DON'T CURSE!!!" ". . . sorry." "Go get me my Dr Pepper. The ice is going to melt out there. Better yet, go to the lobby and fill it with more ice." ". . . okay."

She didn't die that day. If she had I might have skirted all the trauma yet to come, but instead she went right back out there and self-sautéed to crisp for another hour and lived and lived and lived until she was good and ready to go. But that's for later.

That night we went to the bubble-glassed, multicolored lobby bar: the retired couple with the motor home passing through on their fourth margaritas; the bushy-bearded truck driver who knew a few of the other truckers we had just seen off I-10 at some linoleum café with the dusty five-acre parking lot's one blue-green streetlamp hanging like a UFO in the air; and the cook in the back—a lanky twenty-eight-year-old—who didn't know that he was her prey for the evening. She showed him how to better stir the sauce. She made him hold his hand over hers as they flipped a dish in a pan. She asked him who his favorite country-western singers were and if he'd ever been to a proper rodeo. He was toast, as far as I was concerned. I knew it was going to be a long night and that I might as well go back out to that parking lot and see what I could find in the desert beyond it.

Parents are the bones we cut our teeth on, but they never talk about the parents' own teeth. They never talk about the bite that you learn to see coming.

I dreamed about her last night, and I awoke happy but sweating.

Up Until 1987, 1997, and 2013

I WAS BORN TO DRINK. I was birthed to drink. My mother drank exactly like I did, and I was raised to be a man and drink like the male equivalent of my mother.

There was no talk of the spiritual nature of things. No talk of God. Our world revolved around country-western-outlaw, eighteen-wheeler culture, and that was that. My mother secretly went out with a trucker for about eight years; my father feared my mother, so he mostly stayed away. The trucker was often off trucking, therefore I was the man of the house: a responsibility that might have been, to some, inappropriate, but fuck it, what else was there to do? She was all I had.

AJ Spurs used to be called The Iron Horse. It was a country bar and restaurant. If she was home, that was the congregating station. That was ground zero. It's where all the havoc went down. That and Boozie's. Boozie's hasn't been around for a long time. AJ Spurs lasted up until recently.

The biggest cowboys and truckers would drink in there, and my mother and I would be off on the side, watching, she in her frayed jean jacket and permed blond hair and me in my Levi's and shitkickers. Always, and very suddenly, my mother would speak up: "Hey! Why you got that comb in your back pocket?" The guy with the comb in his back pocket must have been three hundred pounds of muscle, fat, and cowboy hat, and he turned around, not imagining for a second that he had heard the question correctly, replying: "I'm sorry, ma'am?" She went for it again: "You heard me: That comb in your back pocket, it looks faggy."

What the fuck is happening? I put on a face—tough—but inside I was shitting my pants.

We are dead. I'm eight or nine at this point and that's it, we're done.

Before I knew it, they'd be buying her free Calypso Coffees she'd ask for: light rum, Tia Maria, coffee, with a little whipped cream on top—a speedball, basically. She had won them over with personality and character and grit and something else none of us could really put our fingers on.

Then the night was on, one of what seemed like thousands.

I'd sneak off for a beer here and there, but I was on watch. I had to make sure we were going to get home by sunup.

Years later, one night in the same place, her boyfriend, a new one, ended up under his truck. We'd had a drinking contest at his urging. "You don't want to do that," my mother had warned him, but he insisted. Fifteen or so drinks later he'd just disappeared, too drunk to find his way back to the table after a stint to the toilet. The owner, who I'd known since I was a kid, had come in from stocking produce outside and told us that he had seen his legs sticking out from under his truck, passed out. "You don't fuck with us," I heard my mother mutter under her breath with a smile that only suggests winning. It was that same smile I saw crawl along her face the first time she came to visit me in juvenile hall. It was an expression she wore as easily as the makeup she applied every morning, but it wasn't something she could wash off.

You can play, but don't think for a second that you're going to come out unscathed and feeling good about yourself.

1968

MY FATHER OFTEN TELLS THE STORY about the day when I was born. None of the men were allowed in the rooms where the women were having their babies; it wasn't like that then. They were brought in after the fact: "We sat in the waiting room or at home. We were the taxis after the water broke. That's just the way it was then."

My mother had me in an hour and a half, from start to finish. My brother, it was less time. She was that kind of person—she just wanted to be done with it, and get on to the next step, the next party.

"The doctor finally called me in with a big, twisted smile on his face. I'd been listening to her from out there screaming louder than anyone else in the hospital, we all did: all the expectant fathers. She kept saying 'GET THIS FUCKING THING OUTTA ME!!!' Going in there wasn't my first instinct, but the doc led me in regardless, and there you were all bloodied and bruised up and your head was deeply misshapen, like a cone. It looked like someone had grabbed it and stretched it until it looked more like an eggplant than a head. It was half the length of my arm. The first thing I said was, 'Put it back!'"

He always follows that last part with a big laugh, a totally exaggerated belly laugh.

I know he thinks the story is like telling me the first time he saw me was one of the great moments in his life—this newborn miracle, this reveal of a love consummated—but it always comes out like he was showing his buddies a turd after a traumatic shit that clogged up the toilet and not even liquid Drano would clear it.

1979

FIRST TIME I WENT TO A DRIVE-IN I drank a beer in the backseat of a rusty sky-blue Oldsmobile. The scent inside was of upholstery cleaner, warm ale, and stale cigarettes. The driver was the uncle of my best friend, Danny. Danny had Scotch tape wrapped around the right side of his black glasses, and his eyes were stuck squinted because of the number of operations he had had on them as a child. Danny, even though he was three years older than me, was my best friend, and my best friend hated me. I mean, he loved me as much as we all loved each other, being that your nearest neighbor was at least a mile away, but there was always something extra that stabbed at him about me: maybe that my father was an actor, or that I was given a motorcycle long before him (at four years old), or that I didn't have glasses (I would need them later for double vision after hitting my head at the bottom of a pool). I don't know, but as time passed, before he killed himself, the hatred seemed to manifest itself in more violent ways.

The film we saw that night was iconic: Bruce Lee's *Game of Death*. Kareem Abdul-Jabbar left a footprint on Bruce Lee's chest, and the beer I soldiered through foamed over every time I took a sip. I had red Twizzlers, and bonbons: vanilla. It was a good night. There wasn't much to do out there in the country—bunch of trees, some horses, and a broken-down Yamaha YZ80—but going to the drive-in on a Friday night to hang the speaker off your half-masted window, gawking at Bruce Lee with beer in hand, and your best friend next to you sneaking looks to see how far along you were seemed like a good way to pass a slow wind's time.

Uncle what's-his-name had glasses too, reddish hair pushed off greasily to the side, and those eyes that only ex-cons have: eyes that saw pain in everything they looked at, the whites always a cloudy red. He didn't say much but he smirked a lot. And the way he brought his cigarette so slowly to his lips suggested he had seen death intimately at some point: a grandmother, a girlfriend, or maybe perpetrating some dime store robbery gone wrong.

I left that summer, when I was eleven years old.

Danny was disturbed, but not much more than the rest of us. It was his father's birthday and the whole family was there. He found out his mother wasn't his real mother. He was drinking. We all drank here and there. It was the country. But he went into a rage that night. Nobody saw what was to come. He went into his bedroom. Tried to sleep it off, maybe. But when he woke up it was still there: a reality in hell. He grabbed a .22 caliber rifle. We all had them. It was our bucolic flag of pride. He loaded it. He walked out of his bedroom door and turned the corner into the living room. They were all there. I had moved away. He had stayed. A trailer on top of a hill in the country. "You think I'll do it?" were his last words, then he bent over the rifle and pulled the trigger. He fell. His family screamed. The bullet tore through his aorta. Blood was everywhere. He was fourteen years old, a time when you just let kids be kids. We took turns pulling each other in the red wagon around the yard. We climbed trees. We walked miles to each other's farms. We didn't shoot ourselves, but he did. He just had. In front of his whole family. And they would never be the same.

I saw the uncle again that next year at Danny's funeral. He was dressed in a tight blue polyester suit with white buttons and a big, pointed collar. He walked up to the casket just like the rest of us had in the blistering heat of that cinder block Mennonite church, and he stood for longer than any of us had before him. I watched him, curious about what he might be thinking, and just when I thought he was going to walk away he brought his fingers slowly up to his lips, just as he had at the drive-in that night the year before, and then quickly pulled them away from his mouth with a slight, almost silent kiss that I watched fall all the way down and into that open casket, landing softly somewhere on a dead, unresponsive boy named Danny.

There was something about that guy, his uncle. I don't know what, but it was there.

1981

HE WAS IN THE ROOM NEXT TO MINE. She was upstairs. The story I'd heard was that she'd woken up in the middle of the night and told him that his foot was on her side of the bed. "What?" It was the middle of the night, but she made sure to wake him completely to make the point. "There is a line, lengthwise, down the center of the bed: my side and your side. You stay on your side. This is mine." She rolled over, lit a cigarette, put it in the ashtray next to a loaded 9 mm pistol she kept on her bedside table, and fell to sleep never having taken a hit off it. That's the story I heard, anyway.

Soon he was sleeping in the little room next to mine. Divorce was imminent.

As I laid in my bed, I could hear the classical music he'd play from a battery-powered portable radio. He would summon me into his room, ask me to lie down on his bed, then he'd put the radio between us and turn up the volume. There were cellos and bassoons and flutes, but it's the static I remember most and that created a silent rage in me so severe I'm surprised to this day that I didn't have some kind of aneurysm. Punk rock felt smoother. Punk rock aligned with days spent with friends as we combed the streets and experimented with youth. We shaved our heads, took LSD, found mosh pits in the night, drank warm Mexican beer, fell asleep during class, leered at cops as they drove distrustfully past, and got up at 5:00 a.m. to hop on our bikes and go surfing before the day started, even if it was flat. We wanted to keep moving. I was a teenager, and I didn't want to lie down on some melancholy bed and listen to what felt like a sermon of last rites. I know he meant well, but I was my mother's son and the need for movement was innate.

I didn't realize until years later that happiness was his primary goal. To me, happiness always felt like just one of many aspects of what made us up, but for him it was everything. Happiness that lasted too long in people always scared me, the inability to end a smile. Every time I see him in my mind's eye, that smile is always smiling, and everything around me goes quiet.

1984 and 2006

The Goonies
OCTOBER

I'M NERVOUS. I've never done this. I don't know who I'm meeting with. A car picked up me and a friend of my father's (now my guardian) and brought us to the airport. We'll be away, they said, for a few months. I'll wash my clothes once a week. I don't have much, one small bag. I always end up wearing the same thing every day anyway, so no use stressing about clothes. This is bigger than that.

People are starting to show up. Richard Donner always has people around helping him, so he walks right inside Terminal Three, where we said we'd meet, with a few of his minions bringing up the rear. With a smile on his face, he yells at us to line up. We do. I've met Kerri, back when I auditioned. She's the only one, though. Dick goes down the line pointing at each one of us:

"Kerri Green: Andy; Corey Feldman: Mouth; Sean Astin: Mikey; Ke Huy Quan: Data; Jeff B. Cohen: Chunk; Martha Plimpton: Stef; and"—he puts his finger right on the center of my forehead—"this is who is playing the big brat Brand. You don't need to know his real name."

We all laugh. This is all a laughing matter, apparently. I can't help but feel like I've done something good for the first time in my life, but also that it might be a mistake that I'm here. I've seen some of these kids in other movies. It's all very strange that I'm here with them, a part of it. I've never been a part of anything other than with people who nobody else wanted to be a part of.

We land in Portland, Oregon, then go right into a two-hour drive to Astoria, a quaint seaside town full of steeply pitched streets and wraparound porch homes. Corey talks the whole time, the same as his character would if he were his actual character, which I think he might be.

The Thunderbird Motor Inn is where we are let out. We go to the restaurant attached to the motel after we are given the keys to our rooms and drop our bags. After eating, all of us debate whether to go bowling or to a movie. None of us want to rest. We have just gotten here, and all the anticipation and excitement fuels us to want to stay awake until we start shooting. We need to spend as much time together as possible anyway. We need for it to feel like a family.

But we never end up going out; we just stand outside the hotel talking.

I don't know what all this acting business will bring, but I like that everyone seems so excited about . . . I don't know . . . everything.

Oregon is beautiful. We're right over the harbor, and the scenery has a metallic vibe, a light fog that's always hanging in the air. Old buildings and harbors (*Goon Docks*) have a great presence: old fishing boats tapping each side of their slips, and the bridge that you can't see the other side of gives off zipping sounds from the few cars and trucks passing over. It's a different kind of quiet here, and I like it. With this group any kind of quiet is going to be rare.

No Country for Old Men

JUNE

Flying in today: small little plane over a vast and veiny landscape. I want to jump out, not because I'm scared but because I want to be outside. My collarbone is broken, and it hurts. I broke it slamming broadside into the car of some lady who hoped I wouldn't be there when she made that left-hand turn off Highland Boulevard onto a side street by Mel's Drive-In. I was speeding from one wardrobe fitting to another, and she came out of nowhere. I felt like I was in the air forever (like this plane ride) and spent the time thinking about how nice it would've been to work with the Coens, and how I hoped the damage to my body wouldn't be extensive, considering I have kids. We decided later, once the shock wore off, that we'd let it heal naturally, allow the bone that had snapped in half freely float until a natural buildup of calcium binds the two jagged halves back together. Only reason I'm able to do the film is because Llewellyn, the character I'm playing, gets shot in the right shoulder. That's the only reason. Lucky, I guess.

The Goonies

OCTOBER

I did my first scene ever with Sean (Mikey), who is a fun person to work with. The scene was touching and emotional, but on about the fifth take we got into a fit of laughter that I couldn't control. I think it was because I was nervous and I really didn't know what I was doing. You think you can anticipate what it's going to be like, but it never turns out to be anything like what you first imagined: the emotions, the scenario, the smells, the relationships, the heat in your head. Every moment is a discovery, the inside of the treasure chest of what you are made of, or capable of, that has never been challenged before (and that you didn't even begin to know existed in you). Steven Spielberg was on set watching, and I think he liked it. He smiled a little bit once. He told me to keep loose. I'll remember that.

2006

No Country
JUNE

While listening to the stories of Barry Corbin at the bar tonight, I saw a gnarled hand land on Barry's left shoulder. A moment of excitement from Barry, then a few pleasantries exchanged and never a glance at me, until I decided to interject:

"Hello. I'm Josh."

The face belonging to the gnarled hand looked at me without any expression.

"Okay . . ."

"I'm playing Moss."

"Moss. Llewellyn Moss?"

"Yessir."

He stared at me for a long time, studying me.

"Josh Brolin?"

"Yessir."

"Well, I'll be damned."

"Yessir."

He looked at me a while longer then started speaking with Barry again about nothing in particular, something about his hair.

His stare was like one I used to use on my younger brother when he wouldn't give me something I wanted. It was a stare of disdain and distaste.

I've watched Tommy Lee Jones for so many years that to be there with him, being sized up by his overtly certain cowboy eyes and that Harvard something-to-prove disposition, I just couldn't help but be rendered quieter than I'm used to and simply left to watch it all unfold right there in front of me. Tommy Lee Jones. Damn.

"You think about your clothes?" he asked my button-down shirt.

"Personally, or the character's?"

(*A short pause, a look.*) "Personally."

"Yeah, I have."

A waitress passed behind us with most of her legs bare, a short skirt far above midthigh. He couldn't have cared less.

"You know Moss is from San Saba?"

"Yessir, I do, exactly where you're from."

There was another pause, a heavy weight in the air as he looked away into a distance as if something was there that wasn't.

"That's right."

I watched him turn and saunter off with a small limp and noted that there were some frat boys on the other side of the lobby waiting to shake his hand, but without even acknowledging them he continued right through them to the exit door, and out alone into a dark, thin-aired Santa Fe night.

He's a cowboy the best he can be, the most cowboy I've ever seen on film.

But when you grow up feeding sixty-five horses every morning, you learn to hate it bad. Five-thirty a.m. is too fucking early for an eight-year-old to do that much work.

Eventually, you learn to decipher between those in need and those who just are there to fill an empty ego hole.

But, shit, Tommy Lee Jones. Damn.

No Country
JUNE

Found a house today. It's quaint, close to town, and has a little hardscape out back.

I had diarrhea all day. It was great. I shat at least twelve times. It's my favorite thing to do. I'd much rather be doing that than working. I wonder why everybody is leaving? Javier left, and Kelly is going back to England soon. I'm not working tomorrow, so I hope that the stars line up and I have diarrhea all day tomorrow too. If I'm lucky, maybe I'll puke a few times, or have blood in my urine. One can only dream.

I miss the family, my kids.

I have a mustache now. Not sure about it yet. Joel was worried it was going to look like I was part of the Village People, that flippant disco band from the 1970s. The collarbone is moving a little less than it was before. The healing is slow though. It's been two and a half weeks.

Something's trying to keep me down. I won't let it.

The Goonies
OCTOBER

Halloween.

I worked a lot today and there were some great scenes. I was in a good mood, which, now that I'm getting used to all this, is more and more often the case. After I got back to the hotel, I got some makeup put on me by Tony, the makeup guy. I looked like someone who had just gotten the shit kicked out of him. It was gruesome: blood everywhere, nose broken, swollen eyes. Halloween. It was perfect. I looked horrible. The cast went to the YMCA, where the whole town showed up. Each actor sat on their own special plastic and metal seat and signed autographs on fold-out plastic picnic tables for at least an hour, one after the other. It was a lot of fun, and I met some great people, even though it was hard to totally connect because of all the makeup I had on. Everyone else dressed up either funny or cute. I might have picked the wrong costume.

I met a great girl there. Her name was Keri. She has blond hair and blue eyes and was as nice as you can imagine a blue-eyed high school blonde could be. I wonder if I'll see her again.

I miss high school. I miss all the people. Part of me wished I was in that line getting an autograph from someone I thought was important enough to wait in line for.

2006

No Country
JUNE

The stand-ins—Funky Will and Roy Orbison (nicknames)—are stone fixtures on set. They are there day in and day out, immovable. Every time I pass Will he smiles and always brings his hand up in what seems like a random gesture: half a wave and half the beginning of reaching out to shake hands but never quite doing it. Orbison, though, stands, face fixated on the plains, one side of his lower lip hanging a little farther down than the rest, and he has dark Buddy Holly glasses covering what might be a thought passing before him.

Me: "It's hot, isn't it?"

Orbison: " "

Me: "Don't you think?"

Orbison: " "

Marfa's Texas countryside is rivaled by only a few other places I've been: the outskirts of Hillsborough, certain parts of New Mexico maybe, and bar none the hills of my hometown of Paso Robles on the Central Coast of California.

On the way back to the motel a storm was passing just to the east, and in its ominous wake was a blue-black stillness under which two red-tailed hawks and one mangy buzzard never moved an inch as we raced past them. They never looked up. I kept driving as if I were home. I looked to the hills to check if I could see my house in California, but it wasn't there. A feeling washed over me that I'm going to live through this movie; I'm going to be fine. It's a good feeling. I know the character dies, but what's important is that I'm going to live. I'm getting better at living now. I've started to prefer it.

1984

The Goonies
NOVEMBER

It's incredible tonight, with the wind blowing hard, tossing the boats in the harbor into each other. A pitch of light from somewhere hidden in the sky reflects off the water softly. The melancholic ringing of bells through the town and harbor sounds off, like they are coming from inside a Hermann Hesse novel, strangely ululating—and fog-like nature towers over this quiet, small, alcoholic town. I hear two men struggle to tie down their boat in chaotic fits. I love being here. Is this what being in movies is: a borrowed life, a taste of something that will never last?

2006

No Country
JULY

Joel came to Mary's tonight a little buzzed. He was telling stories of him and Ethan in the early days: the time they got mugged and one of the muggers sat on Ethan's chest and wouldn't let him get up; how they drove door to door in Minnesota with a teaser print of *Blood Simple,* trying to get money from the neighbors to finish it; and about how Fran won't do press.

I loved listening to him without any filters. He was like watching a good short film that goes on way too long. Things are getting looser here.

1984

The Goonies
NOVEMBER

This is my day off. I'm missing my parents for some reason. It's night and I'm watching boats go quietly by and I can hear the faint sound of a bird's cackle echo. It smells like a sewer in my room. Robert Davi scares me. He thinks he's a Fratelli for real. He looks at me with manic eyes, like he's killed little punk children before. Maybe this is what acting is: believing that you're the person you're portraying? Does that mean that to be good, I have to wear these blue shorts over my gray sweatpants for the rest of my life?

We are going back to Los Angeles soon to work on a stage. They will rebuild the interiors of what's left to shoot so it is easier to film, instead of trying to do it in the actual sea. I get that. The big boat, though, they won't let us see it, not until right before we shoot. I want to see it now though, because Steven doesn't want us to—solely because Steven doesn't want us to.

2006

No Country
JULY

Room 115. 11:45 a.m. I just woke up and walked outside to look at my view of the parking lot. A tickle of rain comes as I walk under the gray cloud cover, leaving the motel door open behind me. Then a sudden outburst of hail and hard water. The parking lot becomes totally flooded and the streets are all heavy streams moving in the same direction.

I think of my mother and how she held that .22 rifle on her boyfriend because she didn't want him to leave. I think of my two kids being born: the chaos of it and that first moment of potential life when their mom and I were waiting for them to take their first breaths. I think of driving alone up Interstate 5: random coyote hair stuck in barbed wire, and the tractor-crossing signs riddled with bullet holes that are strewn all over the West. I think of the time I said no when I found out the girl was a virgin, walking outside, sitting in a plastic chair, and letting my head tilt back while the rain fell hard on my face.

I stand here under this torrent of water releasing from the sky and notice the whole world around me stop to let it happen.

The Goonies
JANUARY

They led us in backward. We were asked to put our hands over our eyes. Several people helped to navigate so we wouldn't trip going down the ramp. "No looking!" Donner kept yelling, and eventually our shoes, our shins, our thighs, our waists are underwater, fully clothed. "Still no looking!" He laughed. Other people were laughing.

They set up the first shot so that we would react to it organically. The plan was to totally submerge us, then from an underwater speaker they'd cue us when to pop up and turn around and reveal this pirate ship of One-Eyed Willy's that they'd taken the last year to construct inside Warner Bros.'s largest and deepest stage.

They lined us up. "Underwater!" We all held our breaths and went under. I opened my eyes and saw a blurry speaker and all the rays of light that were piercing through the surface and onto the pool-like bottom. This was so strange. We'd been wanting to see this thing for months. It all came down to this moment; whether or not it's used in the film was meaningless—it was the lead-up, the experience that mattered. The end of the film involves the ship, and when the ship finally breaks away out of the cave we'll be done, and we'll all go our own separate ways.

"Annnnnnd . . . NOW!!!" The muffled voice traveled underwater. I looked next to me to see if it was time, and all I saw were legs. I pounced up and turned around hoping I wasn't too late and would ruin the whole moment. I saw the ship. It was farther away than I'd thought. The interior of the stage was bigger than I imagined. But there it was: a massive pirate ship in an even bigger body of water that submerged the entire stage. The mast and crow's nest on top almost touched a sky-high ceiling, and there were bits of gold shining from inside the windows of the captain's quarters.

"Holy SHIT!" I yelled. "FUCK!" I wasn't acting. It was me saying this. "FUCK!" Organic. I'd never seen anything like this. It was bigger than life, bigger than my teenage imagination would allow me to swallow.

"CUT! Fuck???"

"Sorry."

"You can't say fuck in this movie!"

"I know. I'm sorry."

The kids all laughed, and even though I knew I'd messed it up, I laughed too. It was a fucking pirate ship built on a stage in a movie studio in the middle of the valley in Los Angeles. I don't know, man. They should've warned me.

2006

No Country
AUGUST

Luce Rains. That's his name. That's his stage name. I don't know what his real name is. He was shot in the throat tonight. He was shot in the throat, then he was shot in the head. He had a lot of things to say, though, beforehand, and, yes, we all learned that he runs the Shakespeare Festival here in Santa Fe.

JOEL: Okay, so I'm going to count three, two, one as you are bringing your head up.

LUCE: Three, two, one?

JOEL: Yes. Three, two, one as you are bringing your head up.

LUCE: But, wait. Wait. What about a bang? I need a bang.

JOEL: Then, we'll say bang. We'll give you a bang.

LUCE: Good. I need that bang. (*Then, to me.*) What if I just pass a joint over to you . . . ?

ME: What?

LUCE: I feel like I should just pass a joint over to you, smoke it, then pass it over. (*I look to Andy, the focus puller, and Andy turns his head away from me.*)

BETSY (*assistant director*): OKAY, REHEARSAL!

LUCE: (*starts to maniacally clear his throat*) Hrururuummmm . . . getting punchy.

ME: Relax, dude. Just fucking relax.

JOEL: And . . . ready . . . ACTION . . . three . . . two . . . one . . . wait! No. Your head.

LUCE: Okay. Okay. Oh, okay. Like three, two, one gargle gargle gargle? Then back?

Ethan starts laughing, turning his head away. Roger Deakins is staring at his little wheel monitor with a look of someone who just took massive amounts of lithium.

JOEL: Just three, two, one, then you'll feel the air shooting out of your head. You won't have to worry about it.

LUCE: GOT IT! Yes. Oh. Gargle, then three, two, one—Bang! Are you going to say "Bang!"?

JOEL: You don't have to worry about it. You'll feel the air.

LUCE: Is this a comedy? (*Luce starts to laugh maniacally while everyone else looks at their feet.*)

Roger shifts slightly in his seat.

BETSY: ANOTHER REHEARSAL! READY!

LUCE: (*to me*) These guys are good.

ME: Yeah. For their first movie.

27

LUCE: No way, dude! They've done like—

BETSY: READY?

LUCE: Fuck. Gargle. Gargle. Three, two, one.

JOEL: And . . . Ready . . . Action . . . three . . . two . . . what are you doing?!

LUCE: (*gargle gargle gargle*) . . . sorry?

JOEL: You can't put your head up that much. We can't see you. We need to see the hit.

LUCE: So three, two, one, hit, bang, then back.

Bruce, the dolly grip, is holding on to the crane and has tears coming out of his eyes at this point, he's laughing so hard. And the right side of Keith's (Props) mustache twitches.

LUCE: (*to me*) I heard about your collarbone. What happened?

ME: What?

LUCE: Your collarbone. You ride?

ME: . . . um. Yeah.

LUCE: Me too. Gargle. Gargle. Hack!

BETSY: READY!

ETHAN: Let's shoot!

JOEL: Let's shoot!

BETSY: ROLLLLING!

LUCE: I'd like to pass a joint . . .

ME: . . . dude.

LUCE: Gargle. Gargle. Gargle. How'd you get this role?

JOEL: Ready . . . and . . . ACTION! Three! Two! One!

The air compressor krflunked and Luce Rains's neck exploded. It hit me with such a shock, such a scare, that everyone behind the monitor laughed. He'd distracted me with the "How'd you get this role?"

For the rest of the night Peter (Special Effects) was spraying blood in my face through a metal pipe. And there was Luce Rains among the crowd of the crew: prosthetic hanging from his neck and head, tubes protruding from either side, looking around pushing constant thumbs-up gestures in my direction and between takes egging me on about how we should do a production of *Othello* together when I'm done with this little movie.

The Goonies
MARCH

We're in Bodega Bay, California, to shoot the end of the film. My mother's here. I had to bring her. It would've been too insulting not to, given I was with my father's friend for most of the filming. She's my mother and I'd be a bad son not to include her.

I told her on the plane that she had to keep a low profile, which she didn't like: "What am I supposed to just do, nothing?" Everything is always in the extreme. My ex-girlfriend left Santa Barbara and the emotional pillaging of our misfit collective: the Cito Rats. She lives up here now—my high school sweetheart—so I'll probably spend most of my free time with her. Staci was gold when I first met her at Santa Barbara High. She had a shine about her that rivaled even those pristine West Coast beaches we frolicked on as kids. She had a purity, and that purity got infected soon after she started seeing me. The Cito Rats were a misfit community and that community relied on themselves. What attracted me to her was different from what attracted her to me. She needed to mix it up. I needed to find a way out. She won.

After only a few days of shooting, my mom called me in the middle of the night. She had gone out with a bunch of crew members from the show. After she got back to her room good and sauced up, there was a knock on her hotel door. It was one of the producers. He asked to come in. She let him. He dropped his pants and wanted to get to it. She's telling me this and then she said: "If you think I'd fuck someone who wears blue boxer shorts, you gotta be outta your mind." My mom. Our producer. This film. There's no way to have her here and for shit like this not to happen. She brings it with her.

Today the producer called me into his office and told me that my mother is sick, and that she may need help. I listened to him while he told me other things about her and that he was concerned for me. After he took a pause to let it all land like a bad actor in a bad movie I said, "Because she wouldn't fuck you?" He asked me to leave his office after he started to shake.

I have a feeling, given I have a bit of my mom in me, that we have no place in this business of moviemaking. It's a friendly bunch, and though the circus maelstrom is attractive, it's not at all like the Cito Rats. At least there's truth in that. We'll see if people like this movie or not, or we'll see if they think I'm any good or not. It doesn't really matter. If it's not this, I'll find something else. Like my mother, I'm resourceful enough.

2006

No Country
AUGUST

It was Javier's last day. They had a cake for him with small two-by-three-inch photos of all the people he had murdered throughout the movie on it. That and everyone wore hairnets on his last day, exactly the way he wore it to get his hair to stay put during shooting. The show is almost over. You can feel it on the set like a wet coat. We are on the stage and the light blinds when you go outside. I feel a headache coming.

Tommy Lee came into the makeup trailer this morning. I'll miss him, even though we never actually worked together.

"Llewellyn Moss is from San Saba County, you know that?"

"I did know that."

"It's been the same for a hundred and fifty years."

"I'm sure."

"It's not a stupid place."

"I understand."

I looked out the trailer window and saw Joel and Ethan setting up a shot. They looked like Laurel and Hardy except both, not one, are painfully skinny.

I wish my mom were on the set. I miss the feeling that anything could happen at any moment, outside of me.

A crew member handed out shirts last week: I BLAME JOSH BROLIN. On it was a photo of my drunk face someone had taken during one of those weekends of debauchery—wearing a cowboy hat and a big, dumbass smile.

I'm going to miss it here.

The desert.

The Dr. Seussian ambience of it all.

The monsoons.

The brothers.

It's absurd, this storytelling business. We are children in a sandbox of toys of our own making. I like it, I've realized, if only for the company of those who are innocently trying to exorcize those swirling images going on inside their heads.

The Goonies
JANUARY

I just read a letter from my mom:

> *Josh, I am so proud of you! You've experienced a lot in the past couple of years. Growing up is so tough and you made it even tougher than it was presented. But you've come out of it a totally responsible put-together person. This tells me you really do love it all. Please try harder in school because you will always be able to use that knowledge. We are always learning, every day. Let yourself give the good to yourself and always be good to those around you. I love you a lot and respect you tremendously. Thanks for showing me here. I had a lot of fun—Love you much, Mom.*

I have to go back to school now. I heard they are doing *Guys and Dolls*. I think I might audition for one of the smaller parts. I'll go back up to see my friends too. I haven't gotten drunk in a while. The last time I tried to light that fire and I didn't know the gas had been on for all that time. My eyebrows are still singed from that.

I'll drink with my mom too. Her coming on the film felt like it fixed when she kicked me out of the house. I went to live on my dad's couch. He was living with that chick in her apartment.

I'm glad she's proud of me doing that movie. I have made life harder than it's needed to be. I know that. We all do. I miss my friends. I just want to go back to what was. I'm a Cito Rat. I always will be.

1972

(A Children's Story)

ONCE UPON A TIME there was a mother and a father and a child
and many many animals. They were a family and the family lived
in a home that had lights, a kitchen used for cooking, and a carpet
that looked like the hair of a shaggy brown dog. They lived in that
house under a sun and a moon that came and went with the days
and nights, and the days were long, and so were the nights, especially. When the nights would come and the moon would shine
and the dogs would bark and the cats would meow and the father
would leave and the mother would rant, and Little Johnny would
simply be.

One night the mother used the phone many many times trying to find the father who was out driving or walking or playing
with his friends or hiding and she was yelling into that telephone
that was black and heavy and never yelled back. Little Johnny was
four years old then and he was at that point an only child, as his
brother, Jess (who was meant to be a girl), wouldn't be born until
during that next winter. But it was summer now—a hot, wet-
weighted, San Fernando Valley night—and the moon was high
in the air looking through the clouds and lighting Little Johnny's
face up very very brightly. The mother screamed into the phone
behind him something about assholes and another lady and hell
and that she was going to light the house on fire if he didn't come

home. Little Johnny had heard the yelling before, but he didn't understand the words so well. He liked fires but not in the house. He suddenly thought of feeding the mother of the little mice in the small, plastic container in his room, the pink ones who squeaked and squealed and writhed. He thought of those babies and how they suckled at the teats of their mother. He imagined himself suckling at the teats of a mother who might hold him softly and make him feel like he was floating in a thick cloud with no rain and a warmth that never cooled. He liked to listen to those baby mice because they sounded like helium laughter, and it made him laugh like he was a part of their family. But for now, he looked at the moon in the sky and the moon looked back at him and he breathed and the breath fogged the window blurry before him.

The mother behind him screamed and threw the phone down so hard that it broke the glass table below it. He was startled by it and he, again, looked to the moon and tried not to shake. The mother ran through the hallway to the back of the house, past his bedroom, to where hers was, and laid facedown on the hard bed with the thin flowery duvet. There was no moon on that side of the house, so Little Johnny waved goodbye to the moon and walked down the hallway after the mother, even though he was scared. When he arrived at the end of the bed where the mother's feet were, her toes pointed toward the floor, he touched the mother's ankle, and the mother began to weep. It was rare that the mother would cry. She liked yelling much much more.

After a long long time the father came home. The lights were off inside the house, and Johnny was petting the mother's head with his little hand. A red hue washed upon the walls of the hallway, and then the engine of the father's truck went silent. The mother stood up and ran toward the silence, and Little Johnny could only hear the soft weight of her steps fade away. The morning was coming because Little Johnny could see the dark blue in the sky right over the funny-shaped pool that the father liked to swim back and forth in while he held his breath. Sometimes Little Johnny would hold on to the father's shoulders while the father swam underwater and, with all his might, would try and hold his breath for as long as the father did. He wanted to be like the father, because the father was big and quiet and handsome, and people liked him mostly.

The coffee mugs that the mother had bought in Mexico the summer before were just missing the father's head as he walked down the brick walkway of the home where the family lived. The glass of the windows where Little Johnny was looking at the moon and the moon was looking back at him were no longer there. The windows were now in sharp pieces all over the carpet that looked like curly brown dog hair and all over the grass that had just been mowed earlier the day before. The mother screamed and told the father to leave, even though the father had just gotten there. The mother was mad that the father had been gone and now the mother was mad that he was there in the home where the family lived. Little Johnny watched and thought how he learned about numbers in school, and he knew that when you have one and one that it makes two. But there was one of the mother and one of the father and one of him and he didn't know what that made. And there was a bunch of numbers on the ground now and he felt bad for those numbers; all those numbers on the ground didn't make more, Little Johnny thought to himself. He liked the window when it was one, and he liked the moon when it was one. And he thought of himself as being one, and he liked himself that way.

The father got back in his truck and the red lights came back on and they slowly disappeared down the driveway. The dogs barked. The mother wiped her nose and opened the cupboards to make pancakes. Little Johnny fed the mother of the mice in the plastic container in his room and put a check on his blue chore chart on the wall, hoping that when all the chore boxes were checked that he'd get the backpack with six pockets he'd been hoping for.

The phone rang while Little Johnny ate his pancakes, and the mother crunched across the broken numbers on the ground to pick it up. There was talking and there was smiling and there was laughter. Little Johnny thought about piñatas bursting open and silly rainbows melting and the crazy illustrations of *The Cat in the Hat* and the sun rose into the sky and the dogs stopped barking and lay down in the dirt resting their long chins on their crossed-over paws. And through the broken windows Little Johnny saw in the distance the moon as she slowly walked down the driveway disappearing quietly like the red lights had done just moments before.

1990

THE PRISON WHERE GARY GILMORE WAS EXECUTED shines as we pass it. Prisons have always instigated some bizarre fishtailing activity in the back of my head. They're alive. Maybe it's wanting to be identified in me: hidden circumstances that have now smashed through the guardrails of my denial and careened over the bridge into the raging cauldron of my own horrible mistakes?

Snow covers everything.

The dramatic change from state to state and their climates make me uneasy, as if the unfamiliar land on the other side of a border is a barrier we weren't supposed to have crossed. Miles into Wyoming, the hills have a more concrete texture. Grays and reds. Mars dust. Eroded but strong. The hillslopes are cut with stark geometric shadows and lights that face us as we drive through them. Again, it is making me uneasy, as if I am in a game that is bigger than me; a game I am not in control of.

In the next sorry town the stench pulls at me as if I need it: garbage-filled creeks, fast food, and plastic microwavable dinners. There's no culture, or the solace of a mirage of anything coherent. A petri dish of self-destruction. We park and walk across a stark lot that looks like it's held dozens of murders. The doors scream as we walk in and whine through rust as they open. Inside, my son skips through the aisles, as an innocent should.

Later, his mother gets a speeding ticket in Rawlins, Wyoming: seventy-five in a sixty-five. We spent two hours in Rawlins writing notes to the sheriff's office explaining why she was right to speed, and they were wrong to charge. These attempts never work with the exception of my mother's, who always made it work with her twenty-page run-on diatribes. She was always able to get out of those ninety-five in a twenty-five speeding tickets. Us? Never.

Once we're back on the road the sun starts to set where the sky turns velvet in deep reds and yellow-oranges. Thick clouds lean against the sun in brilliant hell-tinted hues: vermillion reds; mad reds; blood reds. I almost cause an accident looking behind me, but the colors are giving me something I want to be able to recover later, but I won't be able to. Its beauty gives me the same jolt I get when I watch my boy sleep, but it lasts only as long as it persists. It's short-lived by the sheer fact that things are alive only as long as I perceive them to be, and it's not always that I have the ownership to do so. So it dies, short-lived, outside of my control.

The sun disappears, and I turn back to focus on the road. Nobody is talking. The windows are cracked open, and a tiny whirlpool of wind ricochets around the inside of the car. My nose looks broken in the rearview mirror. The low clouds almost parallel to us thicken. We are going fast. Three people. A young family. Faster than we can.

2004

(COCOON)

I'LL DRINK WINE OUT OF A GLASS from now on. I'll get the glass from a flea market, one that's rough to the touch and pink or blue like old, cheap church windows. I'll hold it at its base and snap my fingernail against its rim, listening for its value, but there will be no value that hangs in the air, and I'll smile. It will be a glass like the ones on the dish rack at Old Man Wiebe's house, next to the peeling Formica table, just above the faded sallow linoleum floor. It will have been touched by those people who work for a living, sweat through each day, and by those waiting for husbands to come home. It will have been used by those having just finished the dishes seeing suddenly their rotund men across the room, in lazy chairs, looking back over their shoulders with eyes of sex and ghost sounds of four-posted pine beds creaking wildly. It will be a glass muddy with a man's hand just come off the tractor after plowing hundreds of acres of oat, lungs swirling with dust. This glass will be valuable only in that it is thoroughly American: accessible, tasteless. I will sip from this glass grocery store wine, enduring headaches long before I close my eyes to sleep.

I'll fill my glass then raise it to those who touched it before, those rough hands of gentle people who blossom and wilt like wildflowers.

1988

"I'M HAVING A BABY," I told him. He just stood there, staring at me, one eye squinting, as if it were being partially assaulted by the sun. "Did you hear me, I'm having a baby." "Not you," he finally said. "What do you mean, not me. Yes, me."

I hadn't gone to jail yet. I mean I had been a few times but not recently.

"When?"

"Summer."

"You're nineteen."

"Yep."

"And you're going to have a baby this summer?"

"That's right."

Why not, I thought to myself. I'd always wanted to have kids for as long as I could remember. Sure, I drank too much. So did my mother, and I turned out okay.

"You might want to rethink it."

"Fuck you, man. I'm having a kid. It's going to be great."

To further this idea that I'd always wanted to have kids, just months before I had been carrying around a small school photo of the little girl of a friend of mine. In a trailer at work, I showed someone the photo and told her it was my one-and-a-half-year-old.

"Aw, she's so cute."

"Thank you. And she wrote this to me on the back: 'I love you, Daddy.'"

"How old is she?"

"A year and a half. Eighteen months."

"And she wrote that?"

"Yeah. Isn't that sweet?"

"She didn't write that."

"Yeah, she did. 'I love you, Daddy.' See?"

"Kids that age can't write."

"Well, she can."

"No, she can't."

"It's right there."

I started to panic at her insistence. She's found me out. I'm a fraud.

"No, not you" wasn't going to take. It's gotta be me. I'm going to be okay as a parent, aren't I? I'm going to show my kids how to do things. I'm going to be the power of example I've always wanted to be.

I had done a stint in jail for fighting cops, then lived in a halfway house for months in Pasadena with fifteen other guys, riding my Harley through a deep chill to our apartment on Franklin Avenue in the nucleus of Hollywood to go to the Bradley Method birthing classes somewhere in the Valley:

Breathe: one . . . two . . . three . . . four. Breathe: one . . . two . . . three . . . four. Now, PUSH!

I can do this. We have an apartment. I'm sober now. I have to ride the bike back to Pasadena to the halfway house after this. Flannel shirt. Leather jacket. No helmet. It's cold. Train yourself to imagine the heat in Hawaii, Africa, anywhere but here. I'm hot. It's not working. I'm burning up. No, I'm fucking freezing to death. Get there. Park and lock bike. Thaw hands. Now, the nightly group meeting with all the guys. Ron, the man who manages the house, is short and stocky. His black fingers are chalky, and the ends of them have calluses, but I'm not sure why other than when he hits them on the top of the table separating us.

"The *hairon* took me down," he says. "I had nothin' left. I woulda sucked your dick if you asked me to, but the *hairon* was all I could think about. It was like water to a man out in the desert with a bag of nothin' but tato chips. You hear me???"

Go upstairs. Get on your knees and rest your elbows on the little twin mattress with the thin, smoky blanket that has been used by a hundred other desperate men here before me.

Dear God,

    Help me accept that this is the beginning of a trajectory I can be proud of. I am twenty years old, and I open to a path that you see most fit. Thank you for this chance. (I can't be a good daddy.) Thank you for this change. (I can't do this.) In your name, Amen.

When she was finally ready to have this baby months later, it was forty-four hours of progressive labor. When he came out, he was a dark blue. It wasn't like in the movies where the infant is pink and already the size of a nine-month-old. He was tiny, defenseless, and limp. The doctor set him facedown on his forearm and started to pat his back with his meaty hand. We were told that the throat can get lodged. Mucus. Get it loose. He just needed his first breath. Meat hand tapped a little harder. The nurses watched on. What's going on? said his mama. What is going on? I don't know. He's not a live color. He's not moving. Why isn't he moving?! This is the beginning for us. This is the rest of our lives right here in this moment, in this room, in this hospital. Everything changes here.

You watch for people's eyes to determine what is really happening. You can't focus on their faces. They lie. The face is a shape-shifter, but the eyes can't sustain a lie for too long, especially if the person cares. So, I watched my son's as I thought about losing him before he was even born. How? Who do I blame for this? Then I watched the doctor's eyes.

They changed. He looked up at a nurse, and the nurse sped out the door. You changed. Something is severely wrong. Everybody has changed. There is panic. It's no longer a question.

"I'm having a baby," I told him. He just stood there, staring at me, one eye squinting as if it were being partially assaulted by the sun. "Did you hear me, I'm having a baby." "Not you," he finally said. "What do you mean, not me. Yes, me."

The day after, the nurses walked into our room. Debby was in the bed, recovering, and I was in the chair, Trevor next to me. We were all exhausted, but sleeping with an infant next to you, I've learned, is not sleeping. It's resting your eyes.

We were handed the paperwork for the birth certificate. I filled it out. Our son had survived. He pulled through. It was just some mucus stuck in his throat that he didn't want to let go of yet.

The nurses checked on Trevor, smiled, then left, taking the paperwork with them. Wow, we just named our child, I thought to myself. For the rest of his life, he'll have that name.

Just at that moment Debby yelled out for the nurses. The door opened and she asked to see the paperwork. There was a suspended moment before she looked up half smiling and half pissed off. "Are you serious?"

"What?"

"You left the *s* out."

"Of what?"

"His name. It reads: Trevor Manur Brolin. Like manure."

"What? No, I didn't."

"Look."

And there it was: Trevor Manur Brolin. The nurses were giggling. Debby changed it back to Mansur.

I looked at Trevor on the chair. Pink. He was a deep pink now: still small, still defenseless, but healthy. The music started back when he took that first breath. I can't define it, but it's a music that will only ever be assigned to him.

I'm having a baby.

Yes, me.

2020

I'VE BEEN ON A PLANE for ten or eleven hours now, and a part of me never wants to get off. My relationship at home is steeping in a muddy tar; the ones involving sex always are. Relationships, they say, confront you with the most vulnerable parts of yourself, and I say I must be an office building of sensitivities.

I look up from my quiet reverie while a flight attendant serves me coffee, and she asks me how long I'll be staying in Sydney. "I'm going to Auckland, New Zealand." "Oh. I'm from New Zealand. The South Island. What are you doing there? Work or pleasure?" "Pleasure, I think." She looks at me with playful eyes. I wonder if she's from a small village. I picture her as a child bringing coffee to her father in the morning, proud. He smirks at her. It's beautiful outside. "What sort of pleasure?" "Motorcycles," I say.

She leans in over her clipboard because it's hard to hear over the hiss of the engines. I repeat: "I'm going there to ride motorcycles for a few days, then I get right back on a plane home." She looks at me with a sense of intrigue and trepidation. "Oh, that should be fun." I suddenly feel like her father.

I look down at my menu I've had open since I saw her taking orders from the people in front of me. "Can I have the muesli with a . . . Danish . . . ? Yes, a Danish looks good." She leans back, jots it down on her clipboard. "Anything to drink?"

Every step of the way there are people doing their jobs. But a lean in, a look, even the subtle gesture of putting down three soft fingers on a plastic tray can feel intimate when you're lonely: a sudden waft of Dove soap or the noticing of slight, almost hidden facial scars.

Getting to know anyone is such a complex geometry. We watch each other like animals of prey: sniffing, pupils dilating, sometimes even laying on our backs as a gesture to safety.

My window shade was the only one open and through it was an almost full moon. My loyal moon. My friend. But I turned around, configured my blanket, and stared at the floor instead.

What gets into us? Two people who thrive and play and adventure. We are so fortunate to volley, yet an ill air creeps its way around us and we sink into a quagmire of brown questions.

Endless relationships of this. Useless.

I will land, fly to New Zealand, then ride a few hundred miles on a motorcycle. The movement and the change of scenery will bring some clarity. The movement and the change of scenery will bring some clarity. The movement and the . . . I'll hold her hand when I get home. I'll kiss her on the lips long and softly, even though our little one will be looking from the ground up at us as if she is being left out. How do you have a relationship after having kids? I've always had kids, and the kids win every time. Sneak in the bathroom? What is that? A quickie? It's too planned. What is this?

My mind moves, shifts, and shutters with every image of what I've left behind. I don't know why I'm flying to New Zealand, lady. I don't know why I'm here. I should be with my wife. I should be with my kids. Why are you flirting with me? I'm looking at the moon. The moon has always been there. She never leaves. The moon has left, but she always comes home.

A different flight attendant returns with items on a food trolley. I follow a cereal bowl as she lowers it onto my plastic pullout table. It's not what I ordered. Her blouse seems pulled lower, so I force myself to look out the window again. There is a perpetual pink on the horizon and a strange geography of clouds below us. All breakfasts are being served by women in pink, red, and blue polyester dresses designed by La Maison du Gant. They all have a bright pink collar around the neck.

I've always been curious what the symbolic reference for the collar is. Is it marketing, subliminally, acts of bondage? And as you're being served tea or coffee, the flight attendant is tilting her face toward yours as she leans over, slightly exposing herself, asking you if you are on holiday, and you are left imagining yourself behind her, inside her, your right hand wrapped tight around that cotton sash like a virgin cowboy strapped onto a bull just about to be let out of the chute. And as she looks back at you, turns, and pulls her face to the right, you see her mouth open slightly, the wetness of her tongue just visible, and you imagine, as flesh prunes in ecstasy, her grinning through her mischief.

"On holiday?" "Yes, I am. Just for three days though. We are riding motorcycles through the countryside: me, and a friend of mine." "Oh! How nice." She says it then pulls her breath away with a smile, placing the coffeepot back onto the top of the food trolley. And with a "Well, enjoy your breakfast" unhooks the break mechanism with her foot and moves toward the gent behind me. She stops. Breaks. Looks down. Smiles. "Hello, Mr. Sullivan. Can I get you any breakfast for today?"

I need to get back to my wife. I need to go home. I don't want to ever leave again.

1975

MY FATHER USED TO DRIVE UP from Los Angles on Interstate 5. He worked down south, and my younger brother, my mother, and I lived on a ranch on the Central Coast of California just below Steinbeck country until I was eleven, when we moved to Santa Barbara. That country back then was raw and only touched by farmers growing alfalfa and straw, and crazy horse people—all horse people are crazy, but even horse people know that.

As a kid I woke up before first light and fed at least forty horses. Our horses. I used an old metal golf cart that held up to eight bales of hay or the green '72 Chevy truck that I could drive as long as I had two phone books under my backside. My father taught me how to drive that truck with me on his lap along the long dirt roads behind the Pozo Saloon, where Willie Nelson and Waylon Jennings would come play once in a blue moon.

He only came on weekends or once every couple of weeks. He'd get into his car late on a Friday night after he wrapped his work and take the 134 to the 101 to the 405, which would bleed up into the 5 just past Tejon Pass and, eventually, down into the much cooler Grapevine. He'd always tell the story when he got home of how he put his top down and turned the heat all the way up, and that way the stars would be visible above him and the methane scent of cow shit would let him know that he was closer to home than to the rat race behind him. Cops never minded that interstate so much in those days, so he'd go a hundred plus into the blacker part of the country, where the fog rolls in but never dissipates and there's always an ominous air because of the said lack of policing. People doing people things. That was the vibe once you got out of Los Angeles.

He'd pull over into a gas station and use the head. He wouldn't even turn off his car because he knew it would still be there when he got back to it: everybody looked out for each other out there. There'd be writing on the aluminum blinders on each side of the urinal that said things like GINA GIVES SUCKY HEAD or I DROPPED MY WIFE'S DIAMOND RING IN THE PISSER. IF YOU FIND IT PLEASE CALL ME and it'd give a number comprised of more digits than a telephone number has.

By the time he pulled into the ranch it would be five or six in the morning, and I'd be just up, readying myself to load bales into the truck and make the rounds. He'd always just stand there and stare at me. Maybe he couldn't believe I was up doing my chores or maybe it was him just shaking whatever fiction he'd just been living down south out of his head so he could get back into the nonfiction that was us. And I'd ask him if he wanted to make the rounds with me and sometimes he would and sometimes he'd just walk into the house and fall right onto the bed as quietly as he could before my mom got up and started complaining.

There was something I always held on to about the way he'd show up and tell the story about being on the road with his top down, going as fast as the car would go, shooting through dust devils of methane that would make any other normal human being gag. There was something about how his face would look so young when he'd say it, like I was the father, and he was the son. I'd listen to him as long as he wanted to talk and wonder what about him would later show up in me.

2005

(Fame Becomes Us)

THERE WAS THE FAMOUS WRITER who, during a table buffet
breakfast in Austin, Texas, suggested that I read a new book called
No Country for Old Men. He's dead now, famous still but, indeed,
gone. I was in the middle of telling him about a dinner I once had
with a legendary actor who fell asleep during a conversation over
wine as we, the group, asked him about streetcars and waterfronts
and the like and other run-ins with other famous famous types
who he didn't find particularly famous because, I'm sure, his fame
so overwhelmed theirs. He only spoke of one woman, with long
nose hairs, a very famous woman, whose name he couldn't remember because his fame so towered over hers. We knew exactly whom
he meant, but to him she was simply a distant memory.

The famous writer looked at me as if he wasn't interested
(which doubled my interest in interesting him), so I told him yet
another story of yet another legendary actor who tried to confis-
cate my mother's ranch right after she died, and that that actor
is still alive and still famous but, of course, one of the few whom
hasn't been canceled, which is super interesting, given he's been
around so long and has an arrogance about him that would've bur-
ied most people today.

But the famous infamous writer was still not impressed, and I
thought to myself, what could possibly be the problem other than

that I, the storyteller at this point, might not, in this very moment on the breakfast deck of the Four Seasons Hotel, be famous enough to illicit the default-worthy, mouth-to-the-sky guffaw that morphs into what might be interpreted as . . . well, ebullience and, of course, interest.

I listed many run-ins with the greats, the very thing that I know most famous people are interested in hearing: parallel stories about other famous people doing normal things that get found out and adjusted into mythologies and stories that keep said famous people interesting and not ordinary. I told him about an actor almost unknown at a certain time and me walking the streets of Vancouver during the days of *21 Jump Street*, drunk, hair combed back, scrolling for girls into the late latest hours of the pleasant all-too-nicely-Canadian night; and, also, about the time I was celebrating with beers with a method-y-type actor with a prominent nose and a famous upper lip in a too-bright Palmdale motel lobby after my last day on *Inherent Vice* (he later, incidentally, won a big acting award for playing an unknown clown, and I thought, wow, how ironic: being a famous actor playing someone who is unseen and almost invisible and getting more famous for it). There was also the time I danced with one of my favorite actors in a Toronto bar and squeezed his buns and he yelled at me and I smiled and was happy because everyone heard him yell at me and that's what I wanted anyway, and there was that time I insulted another actor-turned-director's sweater at the Chateau Marmont, apologizing to his agent the next day (because that's what famous people do: apologize to famous people's famous agents or assistants, not the famous people themselves, who are probably in bed sleeping in or on an important call with someone about some asshole who insulted them the night before). Said agent revealed to me that I had been blacked-out rude to the famous actor in the bad sweater, to which I replied that being rude is part of the game but that it's the perfect time for a Step 9 amends and could he please give me the famous-person-who-I-insulted's number so I could do this properly, to which he replied that I know better than to ask for any famous person's personal phone number.

There was New Orleans, *that* time, when I ran, naked, after a younger, more aspiring actress, into the French Quarter, and hit my head so hard tripping after her that it split the flesh down to the skull while she yelled at me to get my ass back inside but I don't remember that time so well but, damn, do I love New Orleans and the love affair I had with her: the way that town fucked me and the way I fucked it back is etched haphazardly into an elusive memory as I was at the time cultivating what might be considered a worst legacy, an entitled ruffian of ill repute.

And I remember this time in London (it happened so quickly) when another petite, but older, actress whispered in my ear: "Twenty years ago I would have fucked you silly." There was that one too. That happened.

But still nothing from the writer, not even a yawn.

I'm looking at him and I'm breaking down. We sit in silence, and while we do, images of other people who I can't imagine would be impressive to him come to mind. They were impressive to me. That's what I'm left with. I'm remembering. I'm trying to remember men and women who've snuck into my psyche for only the few seconds after they introduced themselves, then were let go like unwanted balloons. But these faces are somehow stamped in me because of what they told me or how they shifted my life with that random, happenstance gift of them. What about the young girl I met when I was eighteen in the train station in Copenhagen? Isn't that important to you? The one who I took for hot fries and who cried when I left on my train four hours later? We fell in love for those few hours, and how she lay on the concrete on her side in that train station always conjures a great warmth and a reminder that not every exchange leaves a scar. And what about that hooker in Paris whose blond hair I can still feel lying softly on my hand. How I tried through broken translations to convince her to come travel with me and I imagined me and her living a life on the road, me writing and her maybe a seamstress or someone working with children. Or how about the man in Ireland who took me golfing near the Cliffs of Moher? How patient he was with me and what a glorious day to be so humbled on. Or on that trip through Cuba with the kids and the old woman who asked us into her dirt-floor home and poured the last of the coffee she had? The kids looked to me for an okay and I said, "We're going to get sick because of the water," but we all knew it was the hospitable thing to do, to take it, and to drink it together with her because we would remember the art of her hospitality forever. Or the woman in Scotland, on the Isle of Skye, who offered the trailer in her backyard to us for the night if the B&B down the street didn't have any beds this late in the evening: "Anything for these two little sweeties. My home will be your home. Just come on back if it doesn't work out."

There is no famous writer I'm talking to anymore; there's just everybody's stories as they struggle and dance in their own plight.

2007

Fade in:

INT. A LIGHT RED ROOM —

Sitting are two gentlemen: an actor and a director named Oliver. The director is in his early sixties, the actor is in his early forties. They look similar with the exception of their respective age differences, and the younger man has a slight case of Bell's palsy.

ACTOR: You know, man?

OLIVER: Ah (*laughs*). There's that "man" again . . .

ACTOR: What, you want me to call you: Sir?

OLIVER: Oliver would be fine.

ACTOR: Why are your eyebrows bluish?

OLIVER: What?

ACTOR: Nothing.

OLIVER: No, what did you say?

ACTOR: I asked if you wanted me to call you Sir. "Man" is a term of endearment where I'm from, by the way.

OLIVER: You said something about my eyebrows.

ACTOR: The blue ones.

OLIVER: What blue ones?

ACTOR: The ones above your eyes.

OLIVER: They're not blue. Wow. You're a tough one. Mean, like Dubya. My eyebrows are black. My mom has black hair.

ACTOR: And you went to Yale?

OLIVER: For a time.

ACTOR: Hmm.

OLIVER: You're going to be great in this.

ACTOR: Okay.

OLIVER: Your face looks fine. A little weak, but fine.

ACTOR: Thanks.

(*silence*)

OLIVER: You want a drink?

ACTOR: Water, please.

OLIVER: No alcohol?

ACTOR: Yeah, they're definitely blue.

OLIVER: STOP it! Please . . .

ACTOR: Okay, I'm sorry. So, what was Yale like?

OLIVER: I've met a lot of presidents.

ACTOR: Hm. Why did you say that?

OLIVER: I thought you asked me if I'd met a lot of presidents.

ACTOR: No, I didn't ask you that. Nothing like that.

(*silence*)

ACTOR: I loved *Natural Born Killers*.

OLIVER: You're trying to seduce me.

ACTOR: What?

OLIVER: I've done some bad things in my life.

ACTOR: I'm sure you have. I don't want to know.

OLIVER: You've been through a lot. I can tell. (*pause*) I meditate.

ACTOR: . . . you meditate.

OLIVER: Almost every day, since 1993.

ACTOR: Hmm . . .

>   (*silence*)

ACTOR: Clint Eastwood does that.

>   (*silence*)

ACTOR: Do you think we look alike?

OLIVER: No, you look young now, too young maybe. I didn't want you to do a Christian Bale thing. I think that hurt his performance.

ACTOR: Christian Bale?

OLIVER: The weight.

ACTOR: I think we look alike.

>   (. . . *silence*)

ACTOR: So, you're a Buddhist?

OLIVER: Of sorts.

ACTOR: That's very Yale ". . . of sorts."

OLIVER: You nail me (*big gapped-toothed smile*). You nail me.

ACTOR: You know, I was in Hawaii, we were on the phone. We had that conversation and I realized something. I realized—well, you know, you speak in abstractions. I guess I do too, but we have a different vocabulary. So, I got off the phone with you and looked out toward the ocean and thought to myself: "What the fuck did he say?" And then I realized with some deducing that you felt like I abandoned you with this thing, this Bell's palsy thing. That you were saying I have to show up, because you need the collaboration, yeah? You see, you have to look at it this way: my career was put into a kind of quarantine for forty-five days, okay? My career was in a Turkish prison, which I'm sure you can understand, and it didn't know if it was going to get out, escape, any of it, right? Imagine: you've been making films your whole life, it's what you do professionally, and suddenly something starts to dictate that you may not ever be able to do it again.

OLIVER: Yes. Yes. I understand. I wrote a movie . . .

ACTOR: I know, but what I'm saying . . .

OLIVER: I was smoking a lot of pot then.

ACTOR: Then?

OLIVER: In Turkey.

ACTOR: You know I worked with Woody Harrelson.

OLIVER: (confused) . . . ummm . . .

ACTOR: Listen, my point is if you saw someone on the street with herpes on their lip you wouldn't necessarily start questioning their spiritual maladies, right?

OLIVER: (yawns) Yes. I mean no, I wouldn't.

ACTOR: So, very tangibly, I have herpes in my ear, and the way it manifested was through a paralysis of half my face. It's simple. My ugly starts on the inside.

OLIVER: Your ugly is on the inside.

(silence)

OLIVER: We do speak differently. The difference with you and Dubya is you have an ability to see inside. He doesn't.

ACTOR: Speaking of Dubya, I was thinking of dyeing my eyebrows.

OLIVER: Why?

ACTOR: No reason. Oh, and I put on these socks, bright socks.

OLIVER: (*loudly*) I like bright socks! (*pulls up his pants leg, revealing a bright red sock*)

ACTOR: Matches the room.

> *A woman suddenly bursts through the door.*

WOMAN: Yes?

OLIVER: No, we were just talking.

WOMAN: Need anything?

OLIVER: No, thank you.

> *She leaves.*

ACTOR: Was she waiting at the door?

OLIVER: Sorry?

ACTOR: Forget it.

OLIVER: So, we have the same socks.

ACTOR: Yeah, and I'm thinking about getting my teeth done. A gap.

OLIVER: Why?

ACTOR: For Dubya.

OLIVER: He didn't have a gap.

ACTOR: No, but you do.

OLIVER: Yes, I do.

ACTOR: Have you seen *Dr. Strangelove*?

OLIVER: Yes.

ACTOR: (*pause*) I'm going to go outside and have a cigarette.

OLIVER: I think you should. I think I need some time alone.

ACTOR: You're going to be great in this movie.

OLIVER: What?

ACTOR: You're going to be great.

OLIVER: You mean you.

ACTOR: No. I mean you.

The actor puts his foot on the table in front of him and pulls up his sagging red sock, then, smiling at his counterpart, takes out a cigarette, pops it in his slightly saggy mouth, and exits the red room, leaving the director tiredly eyeing the closed door.

1987

I'M REALLY STARTING TO FEEL like I have no mother. I'd like to pick up the phone and call her, but I can't bring myself to do it.

I keep getting out of bed in the middle of the night and ending up on the couch. It's from so many years of couch surfing; it's now become habit.

I plan to move to New York when this series, *Private Eye*, is finished. I really don't want to go to Santa Barbara anymore. The Cito Rats scene is still going strong. People are starting to die. Every time I go up there, I go to jail, or roll a car, or get into a fight. I have no friends down here though. I'm alone, unless I'm drinking. I'll fuck any woman and then after I give them some bullshit verbiage like I'm trying to salvage a relationship that doesn't even exist. Why? Are the people I meet as delusional as I am or is it just an act so we can turn on each other when we most expect it?

My mother doesn't want to see me, and my father cares but is floating in the jet stream of his own celluloid-perpetuated world.

This adolescent head: a hamster wheel of the same endless, useless thought processes.

Maybe I should just pick up and call her.

February 12, 1995

I GOT A PHONE CALL TONIGHT from my brother. It was late and I didn't want to pick up. I'm in New York. The New York where the soot still paints the streets and debauchery sings boisterous through alleyways then into a bigger arena of polluted air. I feed off the electricity here, the people: there is grit and character everywhere, and now, suddenly out of sleep, my cells are reacting to a slight friction of a voice I haven't heard in a while.

"Mom got into a really bad accident."

"Yeah, what's new."

"No, I think this one"—his voice lowers—"is really bad."

My brother never calls me. Never. He doesn't particularly like me. It's got to be bad enough for him to call me, but he doesn't sound devastated. Something is off here.

"Where is she?"

"I don't know. The hospital, I guess. It was a car wreck."

"She's always in a car wreck. Why is this one any different?"

"I don't know."

There is a long pause. He doesn't know what to say. I'm tired. I know this is different. I have to get up. I turn on the floor lamp, and the light hurts my eyes. I know my life is going to change. I have a feeling in my chest.

"All right. How do you know? Where is she?"

"Dad called me. I don't know."

"Okay."

"See ya."

I'm in my underwear. Bare feet. I walk out into the living room, illuminated by the streetlamps from outside. I can see parts of the Soldiers' and Sailors' Monument on Eighty-Ninth Street. I used to sit on the edge of the windowsill with my son. The old lady across the street would always call the fire department every time we sat up there. My son loved firefighters, so it was great for him. He was never in any danger because the windowsill was wide, made of concrete, and I always had my arm securely around him. We would sit there listening to the coming sirens and wait, gleefully.

One night a lone guy in full Scottish regalia, kilt and all, was playing his bagpipes. There was so much fog we almost couldn't see him when we got up to sit on the windowsill.

I can hear those pipes as if they're playing right now. I can feel my son's hand in mine. I don't want to call my father, but I know I have to. Stepping forward into this next dimension of my life takes moving. I don't want to move. My mother's dead. I know it. I can feel it moving inside me. Something's different.

"Hello?"

"Pop?"

"Hey."

"Where is she?"

"Paso. Twin Cities."

"How you doing?"

"She's still alive, but there's nothing going on. She's not there."

She's not there. What does that mean? She was chasing her boyfriend in her big Suburban at the time. I knew the guy. I went to school with him. He was older than I was, but not by much. He was tall and lithe and had lots of freckles. I never got it: she

62

was fifty-five, he was thirty. It must have been nice, the idea of being attractive to a younger man. But there was a part of him that resented her. She was a hard woman, and she dished it out often. She would ride people to the point where they'd want to get out of the car. Joyce, for example. Joyce was a friend of hers, and between speeding at more than a hundred miles per hour and the constant barrage of hick rhetoric from my mom, one time she wanted out of the car. Nothing but dust and rattlesnakes for fifty miles, but she wanted out. So, my mom slammed on the breaks, let her out, and she drove away. She didn't *pretend* to drive away then come back to make up. That wasn't her style. She left and probably never even thought about coming back. I'm sure Joyce got a ride from the next trucker barreling by, because within a week they were best friends again. That's how it was with my mom.

But skinny with freckles was an angry tool. Not country, eighteen-wheeler angry but tractor angry, poke-the-animal angry, can't-talk-back-to-father angry.

"You got shit tits. Ugly tits."

"I had cancer, you piece of shit. I had an infection!"

"You're old, though. Why am I even with you? What the fuck am I even doing here?! I'm leaving."

"No, you're not."

"Fuck you. I'm outta here."

They were drinking that night. They'd been to Cambria, and there's a dive bar there that she loved. It's a ways away but it was something different from AJ Spurs, which she frequented much too often anyway.

"Fuck you, Jane. Take your shitty house and your shitty ranch and go fuck yourself."

She pulled a .22 caliber rifle on him.

"You're not going anywhere."

"Are you kidding me?!"

63

Where we're from guns are just part of the living vernacular. Danny shot himself right down the street at fourteen years old. His heart leaked empty. Shit happens in the country, but nobody ever thinks it's because of the guns.

So even though the gun was a threat, it really wasn't . . . until it was.

"Sit down."

"Fuck you!" . . . and he walked out the door. She probably thought about putting a bullet into him. I'm sure she thought about it.

She had had cancer years before. They'd removed one breast and then that silicone implant had gotten infected. They had to take it out before it infected the rest of her body, so she was left with a flap for a while, at least until they reinflated the dead titty. The shame must have been too much, along with the age difference and the romance on a downslope from earlier days when she told me with childish mischief that he didn't like it when she'd tried to put her finger into his butt.

Down the dirt road after him: he in his rickety old truck and she in her bloated green Suburban. He was far ahead, and she couldn't see him. Just past the ranch where I grew up, after the long straight through the hanging witch's hair, and the one sign that was lit up that my dad had helped carve years before, was the curve that turned down and to the left.

There wasn't much evidence of braking. There was only about a foot-long skid impression in the dirt before the tree. I'm sure she was reaching for something and pulled down left farther than she realized as she was already turning left. A typical Jane speed of around seventy in a thirty-five wasn't rare. She hit that tree and that tree wasn't going anywhere.

Old Man Barlogio heard it from his house. It was about nine thirty, and he shuffled to his truck and drove out to the end of his driveway to Vineyard, the main road. The front of the Suburban was crushed. He got to her. His thick rancher's fingers lifted her head. She was barely breathing, but she was breathing still. Nobody ever thought Jane would die, least of all us. She was armored with a character so unique and memorable that to die would be an insult to her mythology. She'd be leaving behind an easy breeze, a cloudless sky, no music on the radio. She was the zap in every electrical current we had felt. She was the alcohol in a mixed drink. She was the wildness in a sunset just after a horrible storm had passed.

But there was blood everywhere, so he delicately put her head down, walked back across the street, opened his truck door with a metal pop, and drove back down his dirt driveway to the front of his house. The black rotary dial phone was just past the kitchen as you enter the living room to the left, resting on a small side table next to his one camel-colored EZ chair. He picked it up and dialed a nine first, then a one, then another one.

She died just after midnight. I told them to pull the plug. There was nothing left. A good friend of the family's, a radiologist we knew, I had spoken with on the phone before I got on the plane:

"What's the reality?"

"She's gone, son. It's all machines keeping her going."

"Where's the miracle in it? Is there one?"

"No. This would be for you now. Not for her."

"Okay."

Then dial tone.

2018

I'M WATCHING PINK AND BLUE candy cotton clouds form below. I am flying north into marine layers and other weather concoctions. I've dreamed this at one time or another, bouncing on clouds (I was naked in the dream), then falling through them: the condensation, the electrical static tickling against my body. Would I zip past someone just stepping off the Golden Gate Bridge? Would we fall together for a moment and be able to exchange a last conscious look? Would we scare the life back into ourselves? Death is a mysterious dream, and dreams are always the most curious sport. I can't fit through this little oval window on the plane though. I've gained too much weight. Would I fall differently if I were in better shape? Now, there's snow. We are over mountains. I can feel how cold it is and I can see the ice forming on my plan. It's too cold to jump now. I'll wait. I'll order a coffee. The flight attendant who wanted to talk about movies will now give me a bit of attitude because I just wanted to look out the window—peace at thirty thousand feet. How many minutes would I fall for? There's something about a winged animal falling through the air that conjures a more beautiful image than that of a pig in a pen, or an elephant with someone on his back, or a three-legged dog in the streets of Tijuana begging for water, everybody avoiding him but talking about it later.

2006

(A Letter)

Dearest Wally,

Okay, I was given the nefarious opportunity to work with TLJ again with that director and said no. Why? I don't know yet, but they are in New Mexico shooting something that is better than not, but the part offered was given to another actor which confirmed my convictions that the role was deserving of someone much more attuned to what it is to be Marlon's quirky friend (let's call him Andy) than to be Marlon himself. I saw no motorcycles for the character, no jazz joints, no "pop" to drink, and definitely no "birds to dig on, Daddy O." People like that director just don't get us, Wally. They don't understand that we are of another time, dig?

Instead, I am home, having just come back from racing cars up in the Salinas Valley. I placed third, twice. I started in the back both times and weaseled my way to third. My only preparation for each race was watching "Play Misty for Me." Don't ask why because I don't know. I only know that it worked like a charm.

I've finished writing the submarine movie (which I think is amazing) and I'm ready for you guys to look at it. It's a bit long right now (354 pages), but we can work on shaving off a few extraneous moments here and there if you really feel it necessary. It doesn't take place in Fargo anymore. It's the little town next to it (Wahpeton), so same accent. Same cast (as we discussed) but different time of year (the snow HAS to melt— I can't move on that one) and I think that we should start in the spring and do pickups in the . . . Blah blah blah, you get it. Totally open to suggestions though. I've done a rough budget and will discuss when I see you (It's a Russian sub and I don't know yet what we can get one of those for, but I have budgeted it in and I'm thinking they may be fairly cheap).

Life is not the same without you, Wally.

Continue to enjoy *Hollywood Squares*, and I'll continue to rev my bike until it finds itself close outside Belleview Medical Facility where you'll be moseying down one of the few streets branching out from there, head down, coming up with a reason not to do my submarine movie because you're afraid that it will be so much better than that movie you did in the town next to the one mine takes place in (Yes, I'm calling mine "WAHPETON"—way better than "A SUBMARINE TALE BASED ON THAT MOVIE 'FARGO' BUT IN THE TOWN OF WAHPETON WITH THE SAME CAST"). Anyway, read it. It's good.

Life is not the same without you, Wally.

I went to Turks and Caicos, by the way, where I severely sprained my ankle the first night there. I gimped around that island with my "testicular problem," my graying beard, my atrophied shoulder, and my leg jutting out to one side in true John Merrick fashion. I am now known as "Boo Boo Brolin." It's sad. I'm a mess. That's why I'm racing again— just trying to end it once and for all.

Send me your mailing address.

Marlon

2021

(Santa Fe)

THE CHERRY BLOSSOMS HAVE EXPLODED overnight. Last night's sleep was plagued: visions of witch hunts, mind frenzies, some form of devilry. I woke up at one point but willed myself back to sleep because the goings-on are too interesting to miss. I should get outside this morning. I need to take in something tactile.

I walk along the gravel, eventually sitting to look at photos of my daughter swimming in a pool while she's holding her breath. She looks into my eyes from the photograph. She was only a few months old. Her gaze reminds me of photos I've seen of Georgia O'Keeffe: the leathery smirk, brush in hand, evidence of her having spent months studying the holes in the dried bones of horses and steers, the choice colors she used for a mesa, the contours of a high desert hill as she stood there watching it all. Her look has a deep sense of ownership. That's what it is. That's what I see in my daughter's eyes.

She holds her breath, suspended in a new and unfamiliar feeling, trusting somehow that these experiences will open her like these cherry blossoms above us that are so suddenly exploding gorgeous, without ever a warning.

2020

THERE IS NOTHING WORSE THAN WITNESSING the fear that eats at your child as they navigate toward their own palette of maturity. That first excited inhale that can eventually turn on a dime. Suddenly, the imagination rages with a clamoring that leaves the softest of them too afraid for the *can*. That given gift of consciousness that slaps and grips the little psyche breathless and renders their ground uncertain and its skies dark and weathered. Their undeveloped life is but an imprisoned bull that sits placid, then explodes once the gate of its potential is flung open, at once flying and angry and kicking and spitting.

There is nothing so pure as the young who are just beginning to awe at that investment of a breath, and slowly, so painfully, realizing how all the breasts of their passions hang in wait, just out of touch. Into their maturity solace will hide with only a yearning scent of milk left in the air; but they are there. It is there: your own sense of character to be cultivated.

Hold fast, my sweet girl, and know that we are here to try and ease you: armor intact, swords drawn, and tears like bits of salt blocks falling down our cheeks.

1976

IT'S COLD. There's a veil of shimmering frost on our sleeping bags. I can hear it crinkle as I pull the bag closer to my chin. I haven't opened my eyes yet. I also hear the ducks running on the surface of the water with that familiar titter-tat from having grown up here in the country. My father is next to me. We hunted yesterday. He handed me a 20-gauge shotgun and told me that we were going to shoot dove. I'm good with a gun. I always have been. I'm steady with violence, but violence doesn't suit me. I envision the consequence of it, acutely: a grandmother squirrel calling for her favorite babe after it's taken one to the head; a panicked fox tearfully combing the ranch as she tries to locate her now-dead offspring; a doe braying for her bambi. The thoughts haunt me.

I downed two with one shot. The white doves now lay dead, wrapped in a plastic bag and tied off.

There's a low fog over the reservoir that sits under the rising sun. We've built a small campfire where my father has heated water, then poured it into a blue speckled tin cup. He spoons instant coffee into it and stirs until all the granules have melted away. When he brings the cup to his mouth, his bottom lip shakes convulsively. It's always done that. I don't know why. I watch it as I poke the point of the fishing hook onto the pad of my index finger.

Last time I was up at this pond, it was with my entire family and a few friends. It was a very hot day. We were swimming, and the adults were drinking beers and ice teas. There was the nineteen-year-old cowboy who seemed to always be hanging around from down the road, the son of the old man who would eventually find my mother smashed against that oak tree on the other side of the street from his driveway. The cowboy son, I think, had a thing for her.

Me and the kids, my younger brother included, had romped around in the muddy algae along the pond's edge most of the day. Suddenly there was a sting at my foot. I pulled it out of the pond mud with a fart-y suction-y pop and saw immediately that there was a thick, barbed fishbone embedded deep into the middle of my foot.

Hospital.

Don't cry.

Novocain.

A couple of stitches.

We hadn't been back to the pond since. I don't know why, but the fishbone stabbing brought with it an ill feeling that nobody wanted to enter again. But my father was bigger than that, and his father had hunted with him, so now was the time to do the same with me: a rite to manhood.

After the doves, I woke up a murderer: a man. And we went to fishing, snatching, and cooking by spike through the mouth and tail, whole.

The fish tasted as muddy as if we had eaten mud itself. "More salt. That'll do it." We put on more salt, but nothing did it.

The fog wore off and the fish meat went mostly uneaten. Once home, the guns were cleaned and put away, one placed softly next to the other.

Doves tucked deeply into the freezer.

2023

MY FACE IS ON FIRE. We've been riding for hours. I'm on my pre-war 1937 Harley-Davidson EL Knucklehead, the hardest hardtail there is, and my body already feels broken. Some reprieve is a '47 Indian girder on front that helps with the rough topography of any of these desert rides. But this trek is backbreaking.

I used to come out here when I was a kid. I spent a lot of time on the road with my mother, then later with my kids without my mother. Now, my kids aren't with me, but it feels that my mother has returned, only indirectly.

In the backseat back then, it'd be me looking out the Cadillac's rear window at the far-off electrical towers and brushstroke blurs of posted red-tailed hawks; and now, it's similar but not as charged as it was then. Then, I'd often see a figure on our travels along the shoulder of the road in California City or Mojave or Truth or Consequences, New Mexico—but there was never a side look, only a deadened stare straight ahead. And it was always a He. Men do that sort of thing: walk away from a family, gamble until destitute, escape from a prison without a forethought plan. It's all on the same canvas: mean, ruthless, and always carrying a backpack of awful negligence on their backs.

I hear various voices, even in this whipping wind. I'm not sure whose they are but I hear, "Look at yourself in the mirror and tell yourself you're okay. Say it ten times every morning—'I'm okay. I'm okay. I'm okay.'" I don't know why I'm hearing this in my head, but I do know it's the status quo talk of today. I can hear it conducting a musical composition of its own ambitious, fictional design. These types of voices prey on the lost, but I am not lost. I am surrounded by the perpetual soft wind of the "I'm not okay" generation being bombarded by hurricanes of "fix it" detritus.

While on long hauls, there is a pain that comes with its freedoms. The significance of that pain isn't to be carried, though. The pain is in the surroundings. It's weaving itself into the fabric of what will become our sense of self, our character.

In a grid, we are thirteen strong. Rooster is on my left, always. We're both in the front. I'm on the right. We're going to the Choppers Magazine Roundup in Virginia City, Nevada. It's 1,200 miles, there and back, and we have to do it in four days. We have to boogie quick through the desert heat and pray that we don't break down. We're pushing our bikes between seventy-five and eighty. My right thigh is burning because the upper exhaust pipe was built too high. At these speeds, it's hotter than usual, and I feel it. I feel it like my bones are over a campfire being stripped, but we can't stop unless we need gas. We can't stop unless we have to.

I should pull over and put a shirt around my face. I can feel how red it is. It's burning. The outer layer is dying. It stings and something in me smiles. I belong out here. I belong with a group of guys who find the personal affirmations of a mirror under a relentless midday scorcher on makeshift pieces of machinery made to last a hundred years. And just when that thought passes through me, my helmeted head suddenly barrels through a small swarm of bees I don't see coming. They slap at me like a barrage of midget punches. I flail wildly for a moment. The pain against the already hypersensitive

75

nerves of my face is the stuff of tragicomedy theater. I breathe through it. I take it. I will not pull over. The stinging, though, increases. It is unbearable. Suddenly, I hear in my head George Jones on the radio and I realize I'm on another desert trip with my mother.

I'm now a kid in the front passenger seat of my mom's car. She has her left leg pulled up underneath her ass-cheek, a fizzing Dr Pepper in the same left hand that's on the steering wheel, and a lit Kool King in her right. The smoke is being sucked out the window at different intervals because of the small dust devils we pass through at a hundred plus miles per hour. Trips back into my childhood toughen me up and when I relax into them, a reconstitution of soaring takes over. I'm flying. I'm almost out of my body, floating over the asphalt. My midsection is at the ready for a bump in the road—tight—but I'm used to it. I'm used to holding everything semirigid. I don't think about it. Everything in me anticipates but is relaxed. All the bikes next to and behind me are roaring spits and coughs in the same key. The pains in my neck and face are gone. It wasn't the battering of bees' fault. It's me who is unnatural, foreign. It is me who is visiting with some sort of ego, worried about what impact I'm going to have during this life. But not now. Pain, no pain—I'm right here. I'm burning, stung, in sync. We'll have to pull over eventually, but for now it's as if I'm happy.

So, as a kid, hand out the window, Mom on the way to take us to a Whataburger a thousand miles away in Texas (just because she felt like it), I learned to love the raw, exposed flesh of the desert. I may have complained back then, but I found that the thing that frightened me most was the thing that would empower me eventually.

I didn't look in the mirror this morning. I got my ass on my bike and took off with a bunch of dirty guys to a place far far away.

2004

WE WERE DRINKING GRAPPA. It's made with the grape waste after the wine-making process, and it tastes like it. You endure a fiery mouthful of reactions when you sip it and feign some idea that you are being aristocratic; the base truth is that you're drinking it to get drunk, so you just deal with it tasting like rubbing alcohol and that it should have been left as the post-wine-making waste product that it is.

I had rented a place with Paul Haggis in Italy in a small lake village while he was editing his directorial debut (and a film he asked me to step down from because I didn't add any value to it): *Crash*. Italy has always held a fascination for me, so what better than random friends showing up during our soirée, staying for a couple of rambunctious days or weeks, then disappearing as stealthily or noncommittally as they had arrived?

After one of the many nightly drinking bouts during those months, a few of us wanted to set out into the Hessean labyrinth of soot-swathed alleyways to see what would ignite. We ended up at a café one piazza over from ours and talking under spooky tungsten streetlamps long into the night, which seemed to satisfy our ghoulish yearnings. When we were good and sauced-up, I told them a story about when my son was sixteen years old deciding he wanted to find out what Scientology was all about, so he took a bus to the Celebrity Centre in Hollywood and took classes. He would call me from those bus rides to and fro and clue me in about the impact (or lack thereof) this "cult" was having on him. He thought some of it was practical and helpful, and some was goo goo gaa gaa bullshit like most make-shift religions.

It wasn't until Trevor made it to the next level and they said he was ready to mentor did a reality rear its ugly head. "I was listening to this woman who had come in desperate. I was listening to her give up all her dirty laundry, when my mentor, who was sitting next to me, slid over a small, folded piece of paper that read: 'Get a load of this piece of work: what a wacko.' That's when I knew I was out."

Smiles all around as I told this story.

Then . . . no smiles.

What?

We're Scientologists.

. . . what?

Paul's wife pointed to Paul, sitting next to her, then to herself.

We're Scientologists.

What do you mean?

We study Scientology.

For a long time?

Decades.

Decades?!

The blood rushed from my face. I looked around at everyone else who seemed to have known this too and either figured that I did or couldn't wait to see me eat shit.

I'm sorry.

No! Not at all. That's a crazy story. Your son. That's wild.

Yeah . . . I know, right?

Yeah. Crazy.

We all sat there, quietly taking sips of our rubbing alcohol.

Years before that, I had been invited to a dinner with John Travolta; Kelly, his gorgeous and uber-pleasant wife; Marlon Brando; a redhead Marlon had met on the internet; my pops and his wife, Barbra (a singer). I was twenty-seven years old and the whole reason I got into acting was because of the early films I had watched starring Marlon and the late James Dean (who, incidentally, died from an automobile accident on the outskirts of my hometown of Paso Robles and ended up in the same morgue that my mother would just months before the fortieth anniversary of his death).

Wow. I was going to meet *the* Marlon Brando.

Marlon arrived late to dinner with a blue dinner jacket, loose slacks, and a scarf around his neck. I don't remember what color the scarf was, but I do recall how stylish a choice it was. I'm going to start wearing scarfs, I thought to myself.

When he stepped from the car and stood up, he reached down and pulled up his pant leg. Under it was blood running down his leg. He explained that he had stopped to help some people pull their cars from a landslide on the Pacific Coast Highway, and when he tried to pull a car out of some mud, it got traction and the bumper hit his leg.

"I just got to the next level!" Travolta yelled from behind a bush, I believe.

Marlon sauntered up to John and John to Marlon and they gave each other an ebullient hug. John excitedly told Marlon how he had just completed a course on healing and that he could help him. John grabbed Marlon softly by the hand and led him inside, toward Barbra's living room.

By the time I walked in Marlon was prostrate on a chaise lounge and John told him to close his eyes. I stood there quietly and left mine open.

John put his hand on Marlon's leg, then his other hand on Marlon's chest. Time passed, quietly. Nobody spoke. I was the person farthest away from them. I watched. Marlon Brando and Danny Zuko. This is insane.

How is that?

Marlon opened his eyes.

Wow.

Right?

Yeah.

I know. It's really something.

Marlon stood up, looking less blanched than before.

Wow.

Right?

Another friend hug.

Let's eat.

I had just witnessed John Travolta fix Marlon fucking Brando. I should've told *that* story in Italy.

1991

FIRST DRINK IN THREE AND A HALF YEARS. I have taken another turn. My brain feels like a separate thing, an engine built by someone else.

I look at the beer. It hisses at me. It wants to save me. I've been stuck in emotional shackles, lost on the hamster wheel of watching my life slip by. But now I'm home, no-man's-land, and I can do what I want. O, these faces passing me by. Nobody is looking at me. O, love. Where are you?

I sip at the froth. I am yours. An acid reflux races up my throat. My chest tightens. I open my mouth wider. I let the froth rest on my upper lip and let fall the liquid behind it to dump into my mouth. I swallow and wait.

I swallow and wait.

I swallow and wait.

I swallow and wait.

Everyone is moving. I want to fight them all. You're dead!—all these dead infecting my eyeline. You know who you are! These disease-infested corpses trotting along: heartless robots walking the streets to and from their work schedules, adhering to imagined lives through the molasses of their denial of what is valid and isn't. Take a picture of me behind my beer. I want MORE ALCOHOL. Exploit me! I'm free! I'm free! I will walk the streets by myself until the sun comes up. I will walk along the red-lit hookers who are so young and I will cry. I will talk to them. I will want to save them and then I will slap myself for being so naive. I'm SO YOUNG! How did I ever get to be this young?! I stay in the dirtiest places, don't shower, puncture myself with messy lead from broken pencils. I am DRUNK! How did this happen? What was I thinking? Fuck you!!! COME HERE! YOU! COME . . . HERE!!!! I run. I jump onto a group of people, young men, friendly, preppy boys drinking wine spritzers. They kick me. I swing wildly. I can't feel anything. Hit me. I hit you. You hit me. Blood. A bottle thrown. I run. I turn a corner, then another one. Cobblestone streets. One light. Shadows. Another sole light. More shadows. Keep walking. Find another bar. Blood on the face. Blood in the hair. Homeless French. More alcohol. I'll share. Share with me. Another fight. I fall in the Seine. I'm cold. I can't remember where I live. I have a child. It was announced today that Eric Clapton's boy accidentally fell fifty-four floors. I'm tossing. I'm cold. I'm wet. I'm on the sidewalk. Where do I live?! I'm so sad for Eric Clapton. I want to go home right now. My genius boy, keep your heart. I love you so much. I am drinking. I am drinking. Pull yourself off the sidewalk. Where do you live? Where am I right now? *"Excusez moi?* Where am I? Do you know where I am???"

1992

This morning I'm barely able to keep these tightly wound
cables from crushing my head:
    of remembering Parisian women walking away,
    disgusted . . .
    and, me, darkly, drunkenly wading in the gothic Seine
My rivers of intention
    all turbid now
    all sunken and stupid
But that will eventually mend
But that will eventually replace
this perpetual dreaming

And it's me I can't stand.

I'm in a war and the final scene
    is of looking out through
rabid, predatory eyes,
    those eyes I spent a childhood looking into,
    of when she put me in there,
    of when invincibility broke.

And I am here now, realizing;
growing up strong you might call it.

Your petty wolves are nothing compared to being invisible.

See me through, until the end.

See me now. Here. Feral. The raw armor of your making.

2000

She had been away for six weeks. Now, he is. He is sitting on the edge of a bed with a floral duvet and a push-button, hardline phone in hand. On the other end, she has a cellular device, which in the hills doesn't get good service. She is pacing around her kitchen. It's a blanch white kitchen accented with random pseudo-Spanish tile that look like thick snowflakes painted by children with flies buzzing in the part of the eye where the tear duct sits. There is aluminum plating on the oven, and on the hood above the oven. There's also the silver waterspout in the sink, and the spring hose handle that helps spray off dishes, which is silvery too.

His view is of buildings. Hers of cypresses and foliage and silver. There is the slight scent of an old folks' home that sits stale in front of both their faces.

HER: I did come to see you. What, are you saying that I'm a cunt and that I never do anything? That I'm just sitting here doing nothing but making sure you know exactly where I am and how much I love you? That's all I do is spend all my time making sure that you know that I love you. You don't want to go to therapy, and I go to two Al-Anon meetings every other day!!! Now you're saying I'm shit? That I'm a bad person?

HIM: You're going in and out. I can't hear you. I . . . what? I . . . STAND STILL!

HER: FUCK YOU!!!

HIM: Can you please stand still?

HER: Then stop making me move.

HIM: I didn't come to where you were working because I was moving INTO OUR HOUSE! I've been in my apartment for six years and it's a big thing to move out, especially after there's been so much friction about moving in for the past two years.

HER: Two days you moved in. That's it. Two years?! What?!! What did I do for two years?

HIM: After Tina and the whole fucking thing about moving in and spending time at my place.

HER: AAAAAAHHHHHHHH! THE PAST! THE PAST! THE PASSSSSSSTTTTTTTTTTT!!!!

(click)

He calls her back.

HER: . . . hello.

HIM: Hey.

HER: Hey.

HIM: I don't want to fight anymore. You act like I'm at the bottom of the barrel, like I'm the one who's at the bottom of the pool pulling on your leg not letting you get to the surface and breathe.

HER: Because I feel like you are. I want to go out but I'm afraid that you'll be pissed at me if I go out.

HIM: How do I make you feel that way? What do I do
to do that?

HER: Oh God.

HIM: Don't fucking do that!

HER: What?

HIM: That Oh God . . . pssstttt . . . thing.

HER: I was just getting ready to answer. Give me a
fucking break.

HIM: Go ahead.

HER: No, you talk. You're always talking.

HIM: How do I make you feel like I'm DROWNING YOU???

   (*click*)

   *He looks at the phone and reaches for it. Goes to
the bathroom instead and splashes water on his
face. He looks into the mirror. There is a crack
in it. He imagines it on his face, a deep chasm
in his character. He looks at it for a long time,
then turns around and walks back to the phone
calmly and calls her again. She picks up.*

   (*click*)

   He calls her again.

HER: . . . what.

HIM: FUCK THIS! YOU ARE A BAD PERSON!!! IS THAT WHAT
YOU WANT ME TO SAY?!! YOU'RE AWFUL. I'M THE ANGRY ONE!
I'M THE RAGEFUL ONE!!! I'M THE ONE YOU WANT TO MARRY?
FOR WHAT? FOR FUCKING WHAT? GO LIVE YOUR FUCKING
LIFE THE WAY YOU WANT TO LIVE IT IF IT'S THAT MUCH
DIFFERENT THAN THE WAY YOU ARE LIVING IT NOW. FUCK YOU.

   (*click*)

   He calls back.

   He can hear her lift the receiver.

HIM: DON'T FUCKING HANG UP ON ME AGAIN! DON'T DO IT!

(click)

He immediately calls her back.

HER: . . . what.

HIM: What? What what what what?!

HER: Say what?

HIM: Say what it is you were going to say after I stopped screaming.

HER: I'm confused.

HIM: . . . fuck.

HER: I'm confused. *(crying)* I get confused!

HIM: I'm sorry. What are you confused about?

HER: About what we're even fighting about.

(Long pause.)

HIM: Did you like the pictures?

HER: Yeah, I thought they were beautiful.

HIM: Have you talked to my kids?

HER: What? Yes. I've talked to them. Why?

HIM: Just curious. I wanted to know if you called.

HER: Why do you think I am such a CUNT???

HIM: Fuck it. I'm done. I am so done with this fucking thing!

HER: Fine. Be done with it. That's what you wanted anyway. That's what you've been hoping for!

HIM: What? How can you say that? What EVIDENCE do you have that I've been looking for a way out?!!

(click)

He calls her back.

HER: What? You're done, right?

HIM: Just tell me this: Why do you think that I think that you are such a cunt?

HER: What?

HIM: Why. Do. You. Think . . . why . . . I don't think you are a bad person.

HER: Then why do you scream at me? Why do you say such mean things?

HIM: What have I said that's been mean? That I came over to visit you?

HER: What?

HIM: We were talking about who visited who. I was moving in. I was moving in.

HER: Oh God.

HIM: What, Oh God?

HER: What do you want me to say?

HIM: I just don't know what you want. I don't know.

HER: I want for you to give me a break.

HIM: What does that mean? You want to live your life? Is that what that means? What does that mean?

HER: It means I want you to respect me.

HIM: Respect how? Don't you hear what I say to you? How much time I spend telling you how brave and wonderful I think you are? If anything I over-romanticize you.

HER: I'm not that PERSON! I am me. I am me. Just me. I am not anyone else but me. I can't be what you want me to be. I am not that person! I'm fucking not!

HIM: If I say you are good—no good. If I'm pissed about something, no good. What is good? What can I do?

HER: (crying) I am not that person. Just let me be a person. Let me . . . Oh GOD!!! . . . let me, just

respect me. Know that I'm not out to hurt you. That I
have to take care of myself and that I'm not out to
kill anybody?

HIM: Kill? What kill?

        (*click*)

*He calls her back. She picks up the phone. They
sit there in silence: the breathing, the slight
clearing of throats, and a mutual understanding
that there will be a time when this conversation
will be forgotten, as if it never happened at
all.*

2016

IT'S LATE IN THE MORNING. A canopy of trees shades us from direct sunlight. We'll be married in three days. Still in bed we lie, awake, cozy, and with all our friends trickling in: excited, inspired, and slightly unwelcomed. I sat up at Mac's View last night where soon we'll marry after the sun dives behind the big granite rock that looms in the distance. I stood there and watched what was left of the sky fade, and with it disappeared whatever more soiled parts of my past I may have been holding on to.

The woods are so nice up there. They hold only the best light shrouded by a canopy of large leaves. I sat watching the silhouettes of the military-straight trunks of trees stand stoic as random wind would shake and tickle at them. This place holds the same mystery as this feeling I'm having of marrying you so soon.

It's personal, ours. We're painting the canvas of this wedding how we want to. And our friends are near, the friends who made the effort to celebrate what they've seen us become in these past few years. I need to make a speech about them. I need to write my vows to you and pull from the roots of who we've been, and the adventures that have been a constant for us, the times when the laugh won and the challenge of how to get a decent night's sleep without searching in the dark for yet another kiss: Costa Rica's dust and sweat; Greece painted white and cuddling in our hovel bookstore;

riding bikes down the boardwalk of Venice Beach, waving and being waved to by all the local help-worms; surly neighbors yelling off their rickety porches at meter maids who were bloated with a false power only to walk away chagrined by all the scrappy locals; the inside of our truck; all the chapels; Ebenezer church; snowy roads through Italian mountain ranges; elephant seals braying on the coastal sands of California; the cobblestone streets of Paris and the spray paint inside Italian alleyways; the doughnut shop in Templeton; and riding bikes naked incapsulated by iridescent Day-Glo onesies on Halloween night. We are the symbolic amalgamation of Black Sabbath meets Taylor Swift.

My love, today, with all our friends and family as witnesses, I vow to carry your dreams with me as I would my own, protecting them as you find your way into making them true for you. I will love you as we walk side by side and take those moments to stop and stow away to remember that we are here today to take on this life in unison, appreciate every kernel of it, every hint of its perfume, and every skinned knee and bruised elbow that comes with it. We endure. I vow to be there with you through all of it: to hold you, cradle you, lift you, desire you, lean on you, whisper to you, learn from you, and always caress our time together.

You are my best friend through and through and I promise, as I have since we've been together, to hold that dear in everything we do.

You are everything I am most grateful for. I am lucky beyond measure, and I would be more than honored if you would take me as your husband from today, for into tomorrow I promise that my love for you is true.

My mother had a watch like this one I give to you and my mother was the most important person in my life. This is a symbol of our timelessness. Each movement you make, the watch winds, and each movement you've made has moved me to no end. I adore who you are today, and who you are today I am so lucky to be able to marry.

Sincerely and with adoration,
Your husband in a couple of minutes

1975

EVERY WEEKEND WHEN WE WERE KIDS, especially on Saturdays, we'd crawl outta bed with a great anticipation. It didn't matter if it was already a melting hundred-degree summer day or a dog-bowl freezing twenty-five, our spring chicken spark as we rolled out from under the blankets was always apparent on those days. Saturday was Hoover's Beef Palace, and we'd throw our boots on, our Carhartt jackets, eyes still swollen with sleep, toss a Ready Western hat on, hop in the truck, and watch the ground squirrels scurry away frenetically as we rolled and creaked down the driveway. About halfway there we'd start salivating at the thought of that tractor-dirty chef's buttered-up French toast next to the two massive eggs, next to the extra dollop of unneeded butter, next to the two (what seemed like) loaves of rye toast and the small mountain of well-done hash browns. We'd sit at the counter while those thick-armed country women would carry ten-pound plates of compost gold from the kitchen to the tables strewn with kids we had just seen at school the day before, grandparents who all had dirty Band-Aids wrapped around at least two of their calloused fingers, and suddenly there'd be a frenzy as we lapped up every morsel of our abundant orders. Cowboy hats at Hoover's were customary and worn without affectation.

After breakfast we'd walk out the back door and across the dirt lot to the auction house and sit on wood-splintered fold-down seats and watch varied livestock be ushered in while the man at the microphone would rattle off sale numbers at Mach speeds. One cowboy would barely raise his hand, then another would gesture, then another until "SOLD!" would, with a hollow echo, reverberate through the sales arena along with the tight slam of a gavel. The woman next to him would write something down in her spiral booklet, and a whole new cluster of cows would emerge. We'd sit there and watch with a slight twist of anxiety on our faces because we thought if we raised our hands, even in a thoughtless moment of scratching our noses, we'd find ourselves driving back home with an eight-hundred-pound heifer strapped to the bed of our truck; and with these boys, that's not something you wanted to get stuck with because there'd be no turning back.

Life at Hoover's sang in all of us without knowing we'd ever lose the song. But the song has dimmed into a memory of an era where hardship sculpted character and the resulting music spoke in a soothing voice you never saw coming.

Country blood runs clean, and clean ain't what this world sings no more.

2001

RAMONA BECAME MORE MY BROTHER'S MOM than mine, around 1974 to 1975 after we moved to the ranch on the Central Coast of California. My father was an actor and was mostly present for weekends in the beginning, then as time went on, every few weeks. Jane, my mother, was obsessed with animals, namely the welfare and well-being of wild animals. She'd spent all of her time around various animals, picking up strays off the street since she was in her early teens. Jane didn't know what to do with the two little humans that were suddenly born and ran in and out of her house at will, but once in a while we'd hear from those gurgling lungs, "Sic 'em!" and you'd know immediately, you'd know if you didn't get on the other side of that shut door within a couple of seconds you'd be cleaning up fresh, bloody marks somewhere on your body for the rest of the day. They weren't dogs. It'd either be a mountain lion, a wolf, or the hybrid of a dog and a coyote: a wild animal nonetheless that someone had the bright idea to pull out of its indigenous habitat so all their neighbors could gawk, praise, and envy endlessly while not thinking for a moment that a wild animal was not supposed to be in a house eating dog food in the first fucking place.

Me, an eight-year-old, and my brother, Jess, a four-year-old, running in and out of the house, our radars honed, and our legs ready to outsmart the most cunning of whatever predators were hidden away behind a couch or a bedstand—but the odds were not in our favor.

"Sic 'em," she'd say, and few seconds later a small yelp came not from me I realized as I looked down to my legs, expecting crimson evidence, but from my brother a few yards away. Then a door would slam twice: once on the wolf, then once more to solidify the barrier between the wolf and my brother.

"Why did you slam the door on Lefty!!??" she'd bellow.

". . . what?" came faintly from behind the closed door.

"WHY DID YOU SLAM THE GODDAM DOOR ON MY WOLF!??"

". . . because it was trying to kill me," replied Jess, truthfully.

"Kill you? KILL you? Love bites, you little shit! Love bites! Open this door!"

". . . no."

"OPEN THE DOOR!!!"

. . . click. (. . . errrrrreeeeeeeee)

The rest is history, as they say. The rest is too gruesome to write about.

Ramona had scars on her ass and in her stomach. The scars in her stomach and throat the doctors found when she went to the hospital complaining of "inside pains." She had been complaining of inside pains for about a month, but it took my mom about that amount of time to believe there was anything going on other than just incessant whining. Ramona had ripped the lining of her stomach from retching so much while cleaning up the arsenal of endless shit that ranged from the floor of the far end of our kitchen to the edge of my mother's bedroom door, which was always closed tight. I would watch her from behind a couch sometimes settling onto her knees with a few gathered paper towels in one hand and the lemon Pledge in the other, and there she'd be starting in on what then seemed a dismantling of land mines during a firefight that was happening along the lining of her insides—she would bow her head away from the fumes so as not to disrupt this delicate danger before her: the hands would start to tremble, a few beads of sweat would fall down her varicose brow and onto either of her bloated, cherubic cheeks; the face would quickly be holding a light vermilion hue, and her Adam's apple would rise and fall with the regularity of a child just about to urinate in its pants. Then it would come, the retching: the lips opening slightly, strung together by a thread of new saliva. The Adam's apple would peak, the stomach tighten, the eyelids lift, the chin quiver, then the hands would expand and float in midair, as if suspended by a puppeteer. The pores opened and let go of the water stored inside them as a warning that the dismantling was deeply unsuccessful—and then it would happen again, she'd retch and retch and retch some more. I would sit there, half hidden behind the sofa, feeling so badly that I couldn't do anything because soon my mother would come out, having heard the retching from behind her bedroom door, which interrupted the test-taping of country-western songs that she was recording with her screeching chalkboard voice, and there would be chaos—utter fucking havoc.

Ramona was our mother for seven years. She left September 4, 1981, sometime in the night when I was thirteen years old. Jess was nine, and that was the last I saw him, for it was at that moment when he drove his personality inside the garage of his brain and closed the door. He did go and visit her on the outskirts of her hometown of Guadalajara a few years after she'd left, but he was never the same. She had her own family now: a baby boy covered with flies under a Swiss cheese roof that stood over a very simple pad of crude Mexican soil. He looked at her hard, secretly begging her heart to reconnect with his, but she had her own family now, and our real mother had the animals. Jess left. He left for good.

The door opened slowly and out peeked Jess's little four-year-old eye.

"Can I stay in here for a while?"

"You know what? You gotta spend time with these animals if you're gunna be any kind of a man when you are a man, which you are not yet. What, do you want to be running from every dog you see in the street or crying when you see a little kitty cat hunting a little itty-bitty tiny mouse?"

My mom would get singsong with her voice toward the end, making fun of the fact that he was a child with any semblance of feelings, and I could see, through the long thin crack of the barely opened door, a tear falling from that one eye, which was by now slowly glazing over.

". . . I *am* a man, I just don't want to come out right now. I've got other things to do in here that I have to. . . ."

I don't know if he even finished the sentence or not. He was mumbling a lot because he wanted to stand up to her, I knew that, but he knew as well as I did that if he did, he would inevitably get turned into a pile of tears and invisible bruises.

My mother was five feet three inches tall, at best. She weighed a measly 105 pounds and she drank Calypso Coffees by the dozen. Calypso Coffees were made with "light rum, Tia Maria, with a little whipped cream on top, please" that soon turned into the incomprehensible "ligtum with a lil wipe cream—AND DUN FOGIT THE . . . ummm . . . T'MARIA GODAMMIT!!!" No owner of any bar would ever eighty-six her because they knew, drunk or sober, she was still the same manic, shit-kickin' bitch who'd somehow find her way in there again and with the frequent protection of their patrons. Nobody wanted to make it worse. Nobody knew whether to love her or to dispose of her body. I think they thought that if they did, if they actually took the muscle and got rid of her for good, that she would somehow make it back, just like in the bars, just like after every drunken eighty-miles-per-hour car wreck, she would somehow crawl out of that grave and haunt them again and again with insults they couldn't even imagine, dodging that bullfrog voice, which seemed to echo through county after county, always looking for a new stud to kill, always looking for a new phantom to strangle, following them forever.

"YOU GET OUT HERE RIGHT NOW AND SPEND TIME WITH THE WOLF!"

". . . okay! okay! just wait a second I have to put my shoes on . . ."

"YOU ALREADY HAVE YOUR SHOES ON!!! GET OUT HERE!!!"

She kicked the door.

"I have to put my shoes on . . . just wait."

Then from the same couch that I would sadly watch Ramona's attempts at wiping wet dung off the floor, and with the worst sense of timing, I'd say to my mother: "Let 'em put his fricken shoes on."

She turned her head toward me and looked at me for a long time with those tired, animal eyes of hers, then finally, with great restraint and resentment, let out the words:

"Fine, whatever you say."

2022

WHEN I PUT HER GOGGLES ON, she holds the lenses tightly to her eyes. I give a tepid snap of the elastic on the back of her head with a smile and start to back away slow motion in the water. I can see by the already-there-smile how happy she is. I take a moment to stop and take her in: her blond hair wetted an easy brown with highlights just at the ends and at her feet multicolored toenails that her mother painted before they snuck into the bedroom to greet me this morning for Father's Day. I look at her bathing suit and how it zips up in the front, is long sleeved, but confusingly imposed with paisley designs. I see how her mouth is chattering, even though the water doesn't feel cold. I wonder if her body, like when she was the baby she so recently was, is still unable to regulate temperature. There's too much to remember. I look at the color of her bottom lip, making sure it's not a frozen-bruising purple. There are so many things to keep straight, so many things that are there to be forgotten or whoopsied: feed, but no choking; toilet, but no sliding off the toilet seat; hug, but don't force it; say hello, and remember that being shy isn't a disease; sleep on the back, now on the side; don't run on wood floors with socks; we can pretend things are knives but we don't actually pick up knives; pull over when you forget to buckle them into their car seats; hold their hands when you walk through subway door thresholds; don't forget what time

to pick them up from school; look out for anyone creepy and remember that it's always the person who you trust the most; and
when you're teaching them to ride a bike, dress them in hockey
pads and run beside them but don't trip or hit a pole yourself.

Are you ready?

Yes. I'm ready!

The smile grows full. The teeth gnash. She takes little ebullient steps forward, knowing I won't move but doing everything
possible to elongate the anticipation of it all. I plant my feet.

Go!

I'm going!

Okay, whenever you're ready.

I'm going!

She says it as she leaps forward in a bicycle run, landing in the
water in the same frozen pose.

I watch her swim toward me twitching, writhing, and rolling
her hips to produce as much momentum as she can. She stretches
her arms forward, but the legs stop working. She kicks her legs,
and the arms suddenly float limp beside her. I realize that when an
arm reaches for a handful of water and she tries to parallel kick in
the same moment, she short-circuits. It is an epiphany. I felt it, as
if it were happening to me. She's three and a half years old. It's like
patting our heads while trying to rub circles onto our stomachs. It
takes practice. It's a learned skill. It can't happen right now, so we
just have to practice it when we can.

The palm of my left hand lifts her from the pit of her right arm,
and I bend down to scoop her onto my left hip.

Wow!

The smile.

Wow!

She's breathing hard.

She's looking back at the distance she covered. The sun is hot today. It burns, but she doesn't feel it. She's still, but she feels manic in my arm. There is a madness in her eyes, and without enough recovery she goes limp, and any grasp I have of her is moot. Her head is now underwater. Her face looks down. She twists and jerks forward, back from whence she came. The fucking girl is a machine. She's my machine.

1997

MY SON AND DAUGHTER SIT CLOSE to each other. The doors are open close by, short bursts of a morning fog have crept inside and tickle at their feet. They eat cereal out of orange soup bowls and read on the glass table out of the *Encyclopedia of the Bizarre*. My daughter, legs tucked under her hips, leans her shoulder against his, keeps peeking at him when he speaks about a family that had the last name 1792 and how they named all their kids after months: August 1792, 8 lbs, 1½ ounces, born June 3, 1963, was one. She gives him a look of wide-eyed surprise, and all I see is how much she adores him, worships him almost. Their history is protected. They look after each other, stepping honorably through the viscosity of this life, parents only a hindrance. They light candles with their eyes. They flame their youth together, always together, traveling through a book of the bizarre, not realizing how absurd it is that he isn't pulling her hair, and that she isn't in my lap, crying.

1981

I DON'T REMEMBER WHAT DAY IT WAS, but it must have been during a weekend. I was over at Jason's, at the back end of the wrong side of the house, in his makeshift room against the garage. It was the same room where later, at fifteen, I made him tattoo me in Indian ink with a crude needle just above the scapula on my right shoulder: JB. That's all it said. Me. My moniker. My brothers: the Cito Rats. Rich Kids on LSD (RKL) hadn't yet started, but it was soon to be. This was pre-that. This was all of us skateboarding and surfing. This was getting a ride from Matt Mondragon's hunchbacked grandmother, Dee, in the blue, rusted Datsun 510 wagon with all of our boards roped and bungee-corded to its roof. Dee was our geriatric mascot. She was our head cheerleader with a walker, and she gave us everything she had, readily and happily—especially her time. This was the late 1970s and the early 1980s. This was when McDonald's was good for you, and when hitchhiking didn't wind up with you kidnapped and kept in some underground shelter for seven years. This was the beginning of a whole new era of angry-adolescent LSD explorers spearheaded locally by us, and it was the beginning of the cocaine craze that none of us would be able to afford and all of us would steal, fight, and fuck rich old ladies for. This was the time where the guys I hung out with didn't run from cops but, instead, threw full bottles of cheap gin at their windshields.

This was the era of the Herb Estate (an actual house where Mike Herbert and his single, drunk mother lived): a spray-painted middle-class home ripped of all its bourgeoisie and replaced with our rage, a rage fueled by all the self-absorbed parents who would rather chew their respective ice than bother themselves with children; we built half pipes in their backyards and stole their cars when they were sleeping to go to the parts of town where they'd sell us cases of beer for ten cents on the dollar. This was before the heroin epidemic and back when Led Zeppelin was considered as punk as anyone willing to not show up at fucking Woodstock. Sid Vicious was a hero and so was Darby Crash. Inside our destructive membrane was Foolish Mortal, Herb, Dead Ted, No Hand's Dan, Bomber, Bohawk, Will Mo, T-Roll, the other JB, Twisty Mole, Mozz, Friend of Fat Chick, Hydro, Scott Doobie, T-Shaver, Hawkzane, Wookie Man, Chester the Molester, Dorbo, Galen, Horms, Car Ride Rick, Shark B, Razor Lips, and Feltcher, to name a few. Then there was The Bottle Shop parking lot on Coast Village Road where we spent all our time and got arrested more often than not. These were the years when we'd sneak out of town, hop in a van, and end up at Godzilla's in the San Fernando Valley ninety miles away, scared, bloodied, willing, and smiling. The trips were well worth the induction into a movement that was as close in feeling to cleaning a wolf's cage at seven years old as I'd known since, and compared to everything else around us, it was the best thing going on.

Every one of us would snap awake at five every morning and bicycle down to Miramar Beach whether there were waves or not. We'd throw our bikes on the ground while it was still dark and walk barefoot on the railroad tracks to Hammond's Beach, arriving at first light. I'll never forget the burn on the bottoms of my feet on our return to the bikes before school. It felt like a torch was blasting them from six inches away. They'd be numb walking back from the water, but as they thawed, that irrevocable pain would surface, and nobody would speak. We learned how to endure a certain kind of pain during those thick marine-layered mornings. We'd learned what punk rock was before we could put a name to it.

That weekend over at Jason's was the transition into becoming bonified Rats. Jason had a sheet of acid, a full sheet: a hundred hits. It was called Red Rabbit and it was known for its heavy-headed, but sophisticated, trails.

There were six of us there. His parents might have been at the other end of the house, but it wouldn't have mattered anyway. Jason wore a look of perpetual mischief on his face. He was a tall, straight-haired blond, and lanky. You knew he was in it for broke; good or bad, he was willing to jump from as high as was needed to assure the biggest effect, and he was always covertly willing that Hiroshima moment—all of us were—but not as completely as Jason. The only other one like that was Manuel Hyde, but for different reasons. Manuel was crazy. He was scary. He and his brother later died in a major gun battle in some field in Hawaii over a marijuana crop. What I heard is that he came out of a make-shift shack with a gun in each hand, either that or one AR-15 in both. That sounded about right. Last time I saw him he had just gotten a cobra tattoo over the whole of his torso—a big poisonous snake ready to strike—which felt like an omen, or a very conscious cultivating of his demise. It was that way for all of us but in varying degrees: we had no interest in suffering through a dead-eyed old age that stared into a past of regrets and wish-I-would-haves.

With the little paper square now basically a piece of toilet paper rolling around in my mouth, I waited on the couch for its effects. I was frightened. We had all heard the stories, the mythology, but Jason and a few others had already taken it at a couple of punk shows, and they'd loved it. Without knowing what would happen and having a brain that was only partially developed at thirteen years old, I sat there and practiced what I thought my trip would bring, which paled in comparison to when the synesthetic effects finally announced themselves.

There were the expected trails at first. Then came the heaviness of the back of the head, like a monkey pulling at the base of your skull. The monkey never left once it all got going. It stayed pulling while I talked with the fireplace and then while I was outside watching the cartoon-laden tips of mountaintops break off, fall in slow motion, and stick upside down at their base (all without sound with the exception of a cough when it landed, that came from someplace I never quite knew). I ran naked at one point down Featherhill Road because I thought it would send me even deeper into what was already a milestone life experience. Deeper. Anything to go deeper.

It was as hopeful a day as I could've had. I had not only weathered the cave that turned me from a boy into a man, but I had also thrived. I arrived at what I thought was a beginning of a happier life.

I don't remember seeing anybody else, but I know they were there. And when I came down after twelve hours, just as the sun had started to set, I knew that life was good and was to be lived and experienced and tasted with a fully protruding, exposed tongue.

I don't know how we transferred from Jason's to Herb's that night, but someone had suggested we do it again right away: trip. It was a new mischief of rats, and only a few of us were left from the phantasmagoric excursion earlier. "Yeah" was all that was needed. One guy saying yeah.

The inside of the Herb Estate was torn to shreds. There were Cabbage Patch dolls stuck feet first into the cork ceiling above with syringes plunged into their heads. The brown shag carpeting hid inside it all the dirt and stains and cum and puke that inhabited it. "Ms. Herb," Mike's mother, I'd known since I was eleven, when my mother moved from Paso Robles to Santa Barbara on a whim. I met Mike when he tried to run me over with a dirt bike while I was pushing my ten-speed up his road, which backed up to the street I lived on. He had wild hair and a raspy voice and always looked older than he was. He'd help us buy drums or drugs because of that Freddie Mercury mustache he could grow. The money used to buy all this stuff was coming from my mother, who was one of the top five winners of the notorious pyramid scheme of that time, which few people actually stepped out from financially unscathed. I was her "counter," but she never told me where she hid all the cash after I had counted it for her. She'd come in through the front door with brown paper grocery bags full of twenty-dollar bills, several of them, walk straight into her bedroom and pour them on the floor next to her bed and say, "Count." She also kept an always loaded black 9 mm handgun on her bedside table next to the turquoise and pink southwestern lamp; rumor was there was a hit list and she was somewhere in the top five of that list. Then, one day, when she was away, I cased the house and ended up finding a loose board on the back of one of her wood dressers. Bingo. At least some of it. All in all, over time, I ended up with about six thousand. With Herb's mustache and a gift of gab we were set to fulfill our whims and debauchery at will. It was me, Jason, and Herb at that point. That was the trio for years.

The second tab started to take effect when a few of us were riding around in the back of someone's car together, Herb included. I immediately knew it was the worst decision I could've made. What had been so great from the very beginning was now its opposite. There would be no revelation tonight. There would only be an implosion, a folding into myself with images of tongues lashing out and bloody babies crying for me to put out some fire I couldn't see. I was dropped off and left at the top of Herb's driveway, facing his house as they pulled away. I wasn't sure what to do next, as I was just into the second hour of this horrific road trip that had ten more hours etched into its horizon.

I went in. Nobody was home. I was barefoot, and I knew there were shards of broken glass littered everywhere. I was conscious and quiet. That kind of silence permeates when you don't know what's coming next, but that something is coming that you won't be able to stop. It was summer and there was no air-conditioning in the house. It was stuffy and hot and my head was burning inside as it tends to when on a second run of LSD on the same day. I looked for a spot to place myself and hold on. There wasn't anywhere that looked like a solace: ripped drapes, tin foil on the windows, holes in walls, stained mattresses with no sheets, broken plates, strewn empty bindles, and lots of to-the-filter burned cigarettes were all I could clock. I was done.

I heard throwing up when I was on the floor later, naked: violent retching. Then something broke, like a bone or an entire skull bitten through by a bear. I thought I'd been alone, and I very well may have. My face was pressed against the carpet, and I forced myself to stop moaning so I could try and determine what was happening. I lay there, my eyes hot and open. I was seeing epileptic faces, desperate children, rabid animals coming at me, all clearly now. It was all true. It was happening. This was hell. This was that multipage description that I later read in *Portrait of the Artist as a Young Man* and threw me into a panic I had never known. The pastor, I think, was relaying to a young Stephen Dedalus the torture of the eternity in Hell represented as a grain of sand: "And imagine that at the end of every million years a little bird came to that mountain and carried away in its beak a tiny grain of that sand. How many millions upon millions of centuries would pass before that bird had carried away even a square foot of that mountain, how many eons upon eons of ages before it had carried away all? Yet at the end of that immense stretch of time not even one instant of eternity could be said to have ended. At the end of all those billions and trillions of years eternity would have scarcely begun." I would be alone forever, in that eternity of Joyce's, with something else in the next room as I lay there as young as I'd ever been. I was again the child I was and all the ramping up into know-it-all status had dissolved and left me like one of those very children I was seeing so clearly reaching with arms outstretched, begging with blood, alive and screaming. I was in that forever forever. There was someone in the next room, wasn't there? My side hurt inside my rib cage, my viscera. I hadn't moved for a long time, as something in me had frozen. My jaw was also sore from clenching the demons away, but I willed myself up once I heard the banging and the footsteps and the toilet flush. Someone had to be in there. Not everything was happening in my head. It couldn't be. There had to be ground, something tactile. Then retching again. A cabinet slamming and someone screaming. An obese man has me by the throat as I walk, but he's not real. I feel him but he isn't there. My lower jaw slacks as the chemicals attack my brain without warning. I stop. I see things. Then they lessen, and I move forward. There is screaming again, screaming then mumbling. I know it's real. I walk around the corner into the kitchen and there she is: a middle-aged woman with long matted hair. She's dressed in chunks of brown bile and hunched trembling over a sink. I'm seeing her in profile. I think it's Herb's mother. I know her. She retches again and a heavy flow of yellows and oranges stream from the hole in her face. The guttural sound echoes through the house, but that is me, I think. I know sounds don't echo like that, but this one does. She finishes and long strands of spittle dangle from her lips as she turns to me and gives me a look as if toward a waiter to give her order, her head slightly tilted up, chin protruding. I stand there, naked, looking back at her. I don't move. I'm shaking. I have to stay here. I have nowhere to go. "Don't," she says and walks away, sunken into herself: a pruned spirit; a shriveled, invisible accident.

I'll go lie down where I was. I'll climb back into my cauldron of Hades and resume repentance for acts unfulfilled, for a life already dying, childlike.

2003

What are my favorite flowers
but those which trick me
Bloom into something other than what I thought.
I am a bee this dewy morning
with you sucking the nectar
from between your petals
And you are opening gradually
Blossoming into a color
that slightly frightens me

2018

I PICKED UP THE PHONE and called Cormac. I later realized I was needing to be associated with a little more character, more talent, more depth than I had been. I have become a society of shallows. He wasn't home, though, so I went about my day.

The next day I called him again.

"Hello?"

I didn't say anything. I thought about hanging up. He didn't repeat. We sat there in silence for a moment.

"Hello?" he repeated eventually, as if he hadn't just said it.

"Cormac."

"Yes?"

"It's Josh Brolin."

"Josh! How are you?"

He sounded frailer, me forgetting that he's pushing ninety.

"I'm great man, really good. How are you?"

"Well, Josh, I'm okay. I'm limping around here and there. It's gotten a little tougher to get around."

I pictured him in Santa Fe. I'd forgotten he was there. I did a whole other film there and two in Albuquerque but never reached out. Why? Our greatest contemporary American writer— someone who if I were able to exchange a talent with anyone, it would be his—and I'd let our friendship wither. Kathryn and

I rode motorcycles up to Taos stopping at old barns and native cemeteries, but we never looked him up.

"Are you in Santa Fe?"

"Yes, I am."

We went on to talk about his son John and the musical genius he has developed into.

"He graduated in May."

"Where from?"

"A school in Boston."

"Berklee College of Music?"

"Yes."

"My half-sister went there."

"Really?"

We talked about how much we love our children; that was the subject of the bulk of our conversation.

"How old were you when you had John?"

"Pushing a hundred."

I remember John when Cormac came to the set with him. He was six or seven or eight at the time. He's twenty-one now.

I didn't want to keep him on the phone too long. I didn't want him to feel like I needed this.

"Well, it was good to hear your voice."

"You too."

But he kept talking. He picked up on my adolescent moment and he chose to be gracious, so we spoke for another ten or fifteen minutes.

"You make it to Santa Fe ever?"

"My son just moved to Albuquerque, so I'll be getting there before too long."

"You should give me a call. Come visit."

"I'd love to."

"What is your son doing?"

"He was working electric, a journeyman, but now he's helping open an event center. He's doing really well."

"How great."

I thought about him not having released a book since *The Road*. I thought about asking him, but what was the point? It's like someone asking me what my next project was. It's not relevant to us.

"Are you still with your wife?"

"No. But she takes care of me. She comes over every morning: makes me breakfast, cleans up, helps me get around."

And that's the type of person I now realize is in my life—all of them: simple, straightforward, and uninterested in nonsense.

My neighbor sent me a photo earlier and texted: "We have a new member of the family." The photo was of a puppy blue heeler, and all over me I could feel driving up their driveway: the dust, the porch, the kids pulling open the sliding glass door; the same door I used to pull open when I was their age. I felt it all.

I listened to the old man speak. I thought of him in front of his Olivetti typewriter writing what he writes: words that come to him like ghosts feeding chickens handfuls of pellets. Not everyone has that. He eats off the dirt of what the ghosts feed his brain.

"It's sure good to catch up with you, Josh."

"You too, Cormac. If I get to Santa Fe, I'll reach out, for sure."

"I'd really like that, Josh. Maybe even go out and get something to eat. I don't get out too much now but if you're here, we'll make it a special trip of it."

"That sounds great. I'd love that. You say hi to John for me. Give him my best, please."

"Will do, Josh. It was a real pleasure. You take care of those kids now. I'm real happy for you."

"Thanks, Cormac. I'm happy for both of us. John sounds like a real accomplished musician. I can't wait to hear his stuff."

"I'll think you'll be really pleased. He really is a virtuoso. I'll tell him you say hi."

"All right. Well, good to hear your voice and take care until I do see you."

"Will do. I'll be sure to do that."

"Bye-bye."

"Bye-bye then."

I hear him hang up. I don't. The phone is still at my ear. I look out at the pond. It's sparkling. The day has motored up. I think about people I respect and what respect is: being brave enough to be fully yourself seems to have something to do with it. That, and not being a prick. That's always good.

2006

BETWEEN SHOTS DURING THE FIRST FILM I did with these two directors (one was a smaller gent, and the other taller than he), we would sit in a circle most times, in silence. Director's chairs, the chairs assigned to each person with their respective job or title or name emboldened on the back, are all, roughly, the same chair. So, equally, we sat there, usually the only sound being Ethan (whoops) humming an incomprehensible tune. The quiet of it all annoyed me. Creative people have things to say, don't they? All the genius that's been bottled up through all the ordinary goings-on of a life, finally get to pour forth on a set, right? But after cut, the labor of setting up a different angle, and a new action, there we were, stuck in a vortex of boredom with me willing the next moment to come quicker.

Eventually, as days and weeks passed, and as I gained confidence, I started to speak up. It was always the same, though. I figured if they were going to inundate me with the same numbing silence each day, I could respond with a similar, numbing unsilence.

"Hey."

They looked up, arms already crossed. More silence.

"I was thinking."

Same. No answer.

Now, everyone knows that the one thing you don't bring up at work, especially during a job you are deeply grateful to have, is that you have a script.

"You know, I was just thinking. I have a script that I think you guys would love."

Arms still crossed, they uncomfortably adjust in their chairs, which slightly squeak.

"It's like Fargo, but it's the town *next* to Fargo. Now here me out. It's cold, winter, like in your film, but in this one there's a submarine. It's a Russian submarine and it's in a lake nearby. We don't yet know who's *in* the submarine, but we know it's from Russia because of the red sickle and star stickered on it."

I'm not sure if anybody has blinked yet, but the little one has stopped humming, and I'm really liking the awkward feeling in the room now and I'm liking the sound of my own voice in such a room.

"Now, it's long right now. Probably three hundred and fifty pages but it doesn't have to stay that long. We can cut it down for budget. It holds at three fifty, but given that attention span has been proven to be way down, I think we should edit to a hundred and five, a hundred ten. I thought we could call it . . . ready? *Next to Fargo*."

The little guy makes a noise, a grunt. I'm not sure what it is but it's something. The one who isn't humming, the tall one, I'm assuming might have had a stroke or maybe just fallen asleep with his eyes open. But neither of them responds.

After about ten seconds a crew member walks by, his steps loud in the warehouse.

I continue: "It's not the only one I have, but I think it's the best one. Think of it: not *Fargo*, but the town *next* to Fargo. Pretty great, right?"

The little guy lets escape a minuscule grin and says that he thinks the submarine sounds scary. I agree with him but add that it's more ominous than scary: "Think King Kong."

Another one of the actors says he has to go to the bathroom and the assistant director walks toward us and says that we are five minutes away from the next shot. The little guy and the taller one put their heads down again, happy for the intrusion. I stare at them, unwilling to let it go. A hammer pounds in the distance, and we are here for months. I'm happy now. I know my place.

1976

MY MOM LOVED THE PALOMINO CLUB in LA. I was eight years
old, and I was there one night with her in some pee-yellow motor
home behind the venue with a bunch of country-western singers:
Mel Tillis, Waylon Jennings, Glen Campbell, Willie, Conway
Twitty, them and all their hangers-on. All of them had beer bottles in hand and whatever else they were doing hidden in their
pockets, and there, standing tall and in character, was my mother:
the bellwether leading the storm deep into a night of chaos, with
her loud bullfrog-voiced stories and mischievous glint in her eye
that was always a primary tool in sussing out the deepest pile of
shit she could coerce the gang into. At one point that night I was
in the little cubical of a toilet in the hallway between the couches
at the front and the bedroom in the back, my eyes closed, trying
to focus on emptying my bladder, when I suddenly heard glass
breaking, followed by loud laughter, a scream, then eventually a
bullhorn with some cops saying: "Pull her back in. Come on guys.
No more trouble tonight." I thought about just staying in that
bathroom the rest of the night because I knew once I opened that
door, I would inhale some mist of a ghost that was waiting in the
air, my future let's call it, a country-western-themed maelstrom
that would forever be percolating a hot uneasy steam inside me.
I put my forehead to the door, still sitting, imagining what was

out there. What it would be like to be forty years old, beer in hand, a new pair of lizard skin boots on, a leather jacket draped over my shoulder, getting ready to go onstage, knowing I haven't slept in days, attempting to clear the rock-hard mucus from my throat? I imagined my future wife having left me with the kids, and friends getting ready to say they were going to quit to pursue other things I knew they weren't. I could see it. I knew it was inevitable. I opened my eyes, zipped together the gap between my little polyester legs, gathered whatever my eight-year-old's courage was at the time, and quietly unlocked the door. It slowly opened to silence: an empty motor home, glass broken all over the floor and Formica countertops, lipstick smears on the white carpet, and four cigarettes still burning in an ashtray on the little fold-out table with cheap metal legs. And like a faraway whisper, I could hear Waylon singing "Luckenbach, Texas" as if it were coming through an old transistor radio with the antennas protruding directly from my head, whose batteries, I knew, would never die.

1990

(Portland, Oregon)

I'M WALKING THROUGH OLD TOWN'S SLUMS next to Union Station SW intersecting with Third Street. Surrounding me are homeless in line for cups of soup; a few of them have valises in hand and I can only imagine what they contain: an unfinished book, maybe; a mother's engagement ring; a tattered sweater of a young daughter who died a few years ago; a knife; three pairs of brown socks; a harmonica; a small jar with holes poked in the top, a butterfly inside.

This is a place where you are left with the nakedness of yourself. It's a baptism. It's a violent cleansing. I feel like I'm on some sort of crusade but don't like the falsities of it. My falsity. I'm looking to be noticed but I've done nothing noticeable. I am not worthy of notice. Even coming here was false. I'm in denial. I'm scared. I have a son at home. Why am I here? Men follow me with their eyes. Is this what it's like to be tracked? To be hunted?

I see five bridges spanning downriver and one is a drawbridge that I don't think is in working order. I'm underneath it, on the waterfront. My head tilts back to where there are also suspended pipes draining overflow water off the bridge splashing everywhere around me, the noise of a cable car crossing over head. The weather can't decide what to do so it stays gray. It's on-and-off rain. There's a hint of sun but it looks like a moon beyond a thin blanket of turbid blue and cold heart colors. My ass is wet from the rainwater I picked up from the doused concrete. The water looks like it has a morbid history, and there's a turned-over grocery cart next to me.

The crossing cable cars send the city quaking. We all vibrate along with them. The streetlamps are on twenty-four hours because of the impaired visibility. Gray skies. Feeling vulnerable. I hear noises: jackhammers and the rumble of CAT tractors far off. I like it here because I know I can go home. A small man with a short beard passes me. He's Hispanic. There is something ominous in the way he follows me with his eyes. This is Boy's Town. It's why I'm here. I'm staying in a flophouse nearby. What gets into my head? I don't know anyone here. I came here for someone to find me. At seventeen years old Arthur Rimbaud was writing "A Season in Hell" and here I am, twenty-two, walking around Boy's Town because Gus Van Sant is doing a film called *My Own Private Idaho* and I want to be in it. If I just walk around, maybe he'll find me? What does he look like? Doesn't he look a little like Andy Warhol? Why am I here? I don't know how to do this. I didn't have a plan.

I should walk back along the railroad tracks, but there is a bird under the bridge staying dry and I stop to look at it. The man who passed me wasn't, in fact, looking at me at all. He's wrapped up in a dirty green blanket under the bridge, trying to stay warm. It looks like an impressionist's painting of a sad era barely survived. The foam block next to him has a swastika carved into it, maybe from kids at one time or another, or maybe from him. Two other men suddenly walk up and sit next to the man in the green blanket. It feels like someone might be stabbed at any moment. I can't figure out what they want from him. They don't look at me but I'm right here. If you can't see me then who can?

I start back to my rented room in the flophouse, and on the way pass a place called Adult Video Arcades. There are men outside, waiting. They are waiting for someone like me to come in. Is this what the movie is about? Runaways. Young kids. Drugs. Parents dead. Getting snatched up. They band together and survive? They notice me with a hunger. I can feel the wanting of their fangs. They were once children, I think to myself. We were all babies at one time or another.

I think about going in because that's what they probably do in the movie. I do. Inside, it is dark. Men's shifty eyes dart back and forth, the blues and whites of the videos reflect off them. Some men hurry from one video cubical to another. I step into a vacant one. I lock the door behind me. I press a crumpled dollar between my two palms to smooth it out then feed it into the video machine. I have a son at home. Why am I here? I'm a fraud. I don't want to do this anymore. Four screens come on the monitor, four different videos playing: on the upper left is a hefty black woman being double penetrated by two small white guys; upper right is a woman, by herself, with a dildo that looks like a *Tyrannosaurus rex*, and it's caked in green tie-dye colors, but I can only see the flat suction cup that is not inside her; the lower left video is so snowy I can barely make it out but I think it's a bunch of silhouetted men with masks on, horse masks, trying to have sex but also, together, attempting to create the sculpture of a horse by climbing on each other; and the last lower right is of two young men touching each other as numbers pop up on the screen telling me that I have limited time left. As I look though my pocket, I hear a knock on the door behind me and at the same time, peripherally, I see something move to my right. I'm scared. I can feel it in my body. I wonder, suddenly, if the man wrapped in the green blanket is dead. There is a hole in the wall, a round hole, and a huge penis protruding from that hole: hanging there, pulsing in little heartbeats. Is Gus Van Sant going to find me in this booth? Why the fuck am I here? I want to be a good actor. I want to have all the experiences of the world. I want to be a living encyclopedia.

I feed the next dollar into the machine. I hear the knock again behind me. I open the door. There is a man. He nods like he wants to come in. I shake my head and start to close the door, but he puts his hand against it. I'm stronger than he is. I push it until it locks. When I turn around the penis through the hole is gone, and left is the strobing potpourri of lights from the video screen. There's another knock at the door.

I'm back at the flophouse. There are hookers and junkies here. I listen to them, afraid but intrigued. I am reading a parenting magazine. There is screaming. It keeps happening but I refuse to check. It's a man screaming. If it were a woman, I'd check it out, but it's a man screaming in a woman's voice, so no.

I leave tomorrow. I realize what I've done here is useless. Mr. Van Sant was never going to "discover" me. I have no connections to these people. I'm not special. I'm not Matt Dillon. I'm the father of a two-year-old. I have this smell on me now, and I don't want to take it home.

I want to go back down to that bridge and check on that man wrapped in the green blanket before I leave. He deserves that. That's the least I can do while I'm here.

1992

I LIVE IN NEW YORK CITY. It's a small apartment with the comfort level of a jail cell that holds for me only the failures of having not survived as a husband, nor as a father. A good father is someone who can work it out with the mother beyond the little irritations and see through the window to a bigger constellation, the larger mall-quilt of compassion. This last fight I ranted down Columbus Avenue with only a pair of red-yellow cords on. No shirt. No shoes. I'd had it. I'd left without any concern for who I'd see on the street, or what I was walking out on behind me. I'm twenty-four years old and I should know better. I'm talking to myself. I look to my left and I catch the eye of Nick Nolte sitting at a sidewalk café, staring at me. Yeah, the guy from *48 Hrs*. I don't know him, but I've seen his films. Spit sits on my chin, and my eyes are wild knowing that I am in the wrong. He smiles at me. I'm no actor of note so there's no way we are nodding at each other like two actors passing on Rodeo Drive. No. He just recognizes my temporary insanity, as if he sees in me what he was, or I see in him what I'll become.

I look away and continue down the street, passing Lenny's Deli and Mail Boxes, Etc. I make it all the way down to the Seventy-Second Street subway station, where Amsterdam and Broadway intersect. There's a hot dog joint on the corner. It's 1992 and New

York City is two years away from its highest murder rate ever. I don't stand out here, shirtless and shoeless. I blend in as just another digit in a city of dirty digits.

I see Philip Seymour Hoffman at the Seventy-Second Street subway station. I know his mother from doing plays Upstate in Rochester, New York. She sought me out after a performance as a young man with traumatic brain injury. She thought I was "a fine actor" and proceeded to tell me that her son was in the city pursuing the same profession. "Oh, good! What's his name?" "Philip. Phil." "Well, good luck to him. Fingers crossed." She is stout and rotund like Phil. Phil, who is the darling of New York and Hollywood now. The Phil everybody is talking about. Phil-Phil.

"Hey, Phil!"

He looks at me shirtless and shoeless but doesn't for a second acknowledge the fact.

"Hey, man," he answers then looks away.

There was never a plan. Maybe that was the problem. I never devised a plan for work, for life, or to be the best at anything. I was a wanderer. I was a vagabond looking more for experiences about life than about what might help my career. I didn't even like acting that much. My interest was based more in curiosities and fears: What makes people tick, and why is everybody so fucking weird all the time?

"Hey, Debby says hi."

He doesn't understand.

"Alice," I say. "Debby is her personal name, but professionally she's Alice. Trevor's mom."

"Oh! Tell her I said hi. How's your son doing?"

"Good! Good! He's growing so *fast*. He's really growing up fast."

"I bet!"

He's talking to me, but one of his two feet is already pointed in the direction that he wants to go, so he's standing there like Charlie Chaplin.

"How are you? You're doing so well, man. SO well. You're really killing it."

"Thanks, Josh."

"Yeah."

"You good?"

"I am. Real good. Real good."

We stand there next to the subway entrance looking at each other as if one is the illegitimate son of the other. We both have the same look for two totally different reasons. And I keep imagining his mother looking up to him with an unadulterated pride and squeaky joy.

He breaks and looks down. "Great to see you."

"You too."

"Make sure to say hi to Alice for me. Sorry, Debby. Debby, because I always knew her as her actress name, Alice."

They were in Poland together. For each of them, it was their first film. That's all I knew. But that's what you do with people who you know are only on an upward trajectory. You imagine that they had sex with your wife, or all your girlfriends you've ever had, for that matter. You think their every move is to defy you, and you want them to trip and bleed and be human on the bottom of your shoe. I wanted him to be as fucked up as I was.

"All right, Josh. See you later."

"Say hello to your mom for me."

"I will."

I look around. It's hot. Midday. Humid. There are people all over the place. There is sweat all over my bare chest. I look back to the subway stairwell, but he's already gone. I know he's sober. I'm not anymore. He knows that too. I could tell by the way he looked at me as someone who just didn't get it, who felt it more necessary to please himself than take care of the bigger picture like a child or a wife. I don't live with my family anymore. I live by myself in a rented cell on the corner of Ninety-Fourth and West End. I need to get back to them. Trevor's probably cooking something with his mom—making a grilled cheese sandwich. I can see it. I need to get back to them. I'm going to miss it all. I turn and look up Amsterdam Avenue. I see blocks of people crossing the street, all in unison. There are no trees here. There's no oxygen.

I look for Nick Nolte on my way back. I want to see him one more time, leave a different impression: as a sane person, only one with no shirt and no shoes. But I never see him again until years later.

It's a big city, and it's dangerous. Times Square still has Jimmy Breslin's face: pockmarks and bushy brows comb the streets daily. It isn't yet the digital Disneyland that it will become. A second-floor walkup is still a shlep in New York. Anything can happen on those stairs. I knock on the door. It's well past bedtime. She opens it. I stand there looking at her. She has a crumpled-up shirt in her hand and throws it at me, then she shuts the door in exactly the same way she had opened it.

I don't move. I refuse to move.

2013

IT'S LATE AND SHE'S DRUNK. I have to put food in her. There has to be someplace still open. Earlier, she got into a scuffle with a Costa Rican girl at some sweaty, oversexed dive bar. The juice gives you that false sense of confidence, that "wish I would have said" thing that's supposed to come after a tense run-in, but you say it. You don't do that. Not here.

"Are you looking at my fucking man?!"

"What did you say, bitch?"

The girl's lilt rides along the same trajectory as her incredulity. She is dark and has fierce eyes and has thick legs and knows innately how to ground herself in violence.

But that was before. Now, we're close to the hotel and we're okay. The president of China is in town, so the main boulevard around the corner has been cordoned off. Nobody's around. We search for food. Drunk food. She needs to eat something.

T-Roll, my buddy, told us not to go out, not past twelve. That's the deadline. Up until then you can get away with most things, but after midnight, you're on your own. I'm not sure what time it is.

About a block and a half from the hotel there is a McDonald's then a KFC on the other side of the street and another fifty feet down. She stops and looks around. "I don't want to be out here," she says.

"We have to get something to eat," I tell her. "We have to put something in your gut."

"I don't want to be out here, though. It's too quiet."

We stand there for a moment, paralyzed, and waiting for direction.

"I don't want to be out here." She repeats herself.

You can hear streetlights shift from green to yellow to red and in the distance there are footsteps of high heel shoes. But those were the only sounds other than our American naiveté echoing through the emptiness of the night.

Her eyes are heavy. She's drunk. She wants to go back to the room. She feels unsafe.

"*Tienes cigarro?*" A voice.

"What?"

She had started to walk to the hotel. I was hungry now. We had survived the night and we're going to be okay.

"*Tienes cigarro, jefe?*" Again.

I am focused on her. I don't have a cigarette. I don't have a cigarette. I don't have anything on me. Where is she going?

"*Tienes dinero?*"

I don't want to lose sight of her. No, I don't have any money. What? I don't have any . . .

I feel a slap on my stomach.

I look down and see the blood start to creep out from between my fingers. I look up at him and see his wild eyes. He is on something. His eyeballs are shaking, they are visibly shuttering. He holds a knife and the knife has blood covering the top half of the blade. He's stabbed me. He's fucking stabbed me.

The yell I hear is as if someone else is yelling it. It's the yell of someone who knows they are going to die.

RUN!!!

She looks back at me. I have to get to her. She looks at me

smiling. She doesn't know what is going on. She thinks my yell is a joke.

I look down at what was my white shirt, and the bottom half is now saturated in vermillion red. I think of my children back home. I think of Trevor when he was born and of Eden cutting her own hair when she was four. I can feel their hugs. I can hear them falling asleep next to me by how their breathing changes.

I look over my right shoulder. There are two guys now, both with knives, and they are running toward us. I lift her up off the ground where she's fallen and push her forward toward the hotel, then turn to face them. My mind is short-circuiting. I don't feel anything. I know this is it. She is running now. She looks back over her shoulder again, this time not smiling. She's seen the blood.

There is yelling again. It's outside of myself, but this time it isn't me. There are two men running toward us from a different direction. They are yelling in Spanish. I don't know if I'm being ambushed. The two men with knives stop, then turn and immediately take off down the empty street. I don't know what's happening.

I lift my shirt to look at the wound and I see where he has stabbed me: directly in the belly button. Spot on. They told me later in the operating room that it's what saved me. The umbilical ligament is the densest ligament in the body and slowed the knife down enough to stop it from hitting any vitals.

Kathryn goes into the hotel and gets my phone. I call my ex, the mother of my kids. I tell her what happened, and she, without ever changing the tone in her voice, says, "I know what to do, but you're going to be fine." Yeah, but I don't know that for sure. She says it again: "I know what to do, but you'll be fine." She'll talk to the kids about what I most loved about them, about what they meant to me, and how I know they will grow into a future that they can feel proud of, and not spiral in shame because of. She knows, and I trust she knows.

I'm sitting on a small two-foot wall along the sidewalk. Kathryn is freaking out because the ambulance still isn't there. A couple of street cops show up and the more she freaks out, the more it looks like they are going to take her in. It's like my whole life is spent trying to get the attention of others but something absurd happens instead.

We heard the sirens far off. They were getting closer. I wasn't dead, so that was a good sign. I could see the blue and red lights reflected softly off the concrete buildings close by and then I heard the van that was just approaching suddenly pass us. Kathryn started screaming again. She was furious. I was positive the cops were going to take her to jail.

Once it found us, they laid me down on a gurney and the wheels folded underneath as they pushed me into the ambulance. Inside one of the EMTs asked Kathryn to put on her seat belt, but she didn't.

They turned a sharp corner and Kathryn went flying from one side of the inside of that metal box to the other, then slid down like a Wile E. Coyote in a Road Runner cartoon. The EMT asked her to please put her seat belt on. We still had farther to go. We had to be calm. We had to be normal. We had to pretend like it was all okay.

In the hospital, the cops came the next day. My stomach was distended, and the pain was severe. To do exploratory surgery you have to distend the area, then you fart it back to normal over the next couple of days. "Stay on your knees most of the time today. You must poot."

These cops looked like felons. They all had guns in holsters and deep-set eyes. The translator thought we could do a movie together. He wanted me to make a commitment. "You and me will be like you in *American Gangster*! *Sicario*! Look at my guys. Looks that could kill, right? Cop looks!"

"What about the guy who stabbed me?"

"Yeah! Yeah! Yeah! We know who he is. The guy from the KFC across the street saw it. We know who it is."

"You do?"

"Yeah. Will you come back and testify? Most people don't."

"Well, don't most people die?"

"Sometimes, yeah."

"Yeah, I'd be willing to come back. What if I had been a woman or a kid."

"Okay! Then we get to see you again and we can decide on our movie! You play a cop! *Sicario!*"

We stayed for a day or two then flew home to start *Inherent Vice* for Paul Thomas Anderson. I had written him that I might not be in a condition conducive to what he might need from me to do for his film, but everyone went with it in stride. It's me, I forgot. People seemed to just accept that what happened was part of my deal. Really? Getting stabbed was just "part of my deal"? I was putting people in danger. I was a menace. This wasn't my fault, but still I had created the whole thing, the big picture of chaos that defined my life.

The first scene I had in Paul's film was when Doc was walking out of a house and I was standing next to my car in the driveway. He tries to walk by me but I proceed to stomp him. I lift him up, throw him against the car, then stomp and knee him while he's on the ground. I thought the stitches were going to rip apart. The pain was searing in my gut, in my head.

Kathryn watched it from behind the camera somewhere. Between shots while I quietly recovered we were already planning our next trip. "What about Costa Rica again?" I asked. And she looked at me smiling and answered: "I know you're serious."

I couldn't just leave well enough alone. It haunted me, what happened, and whatever haunted me I had to confront again and again until it either killed me or ceased to have that power.

"Costa Rica, it is then."

1989

I HAVE A TWEED COAT ON. I bought it for cheap from some roadside retailer. I'm in Ireland and I'm lost. Heading outside of Dublin, I hitchhiked west and found myself in a field walking aimlessly as the sun fell behind a green hill where Holstein cows were grazing. There are ghosts here. I feel people walking through me, as I follow along country roads. My feet hurt, but it's all part of the story, something I'll be able to give out animatedly at a dinner in years to come. For now, I travel with voices that I can't hear so well, voices that have been here much longer than I, and have for years been traveling as aimlessly as I am.

I came here to study the Irish; more specifically, I came here to study Irish priests. I am preparing to act in my first professional play, at the Geva Theatre in Rochester, New York. The subscribers are mostly octogenarians. It'll be a good start for me, trying to keep geriatrics awake.

For now though, I haven't seen a priest yet. I'm too scared to try. What do I do, walk into a church and tell them I'm going to play one of them? What is one of them?

I sleep in a field that night, my tweed coat draped over me. It's cold. I hear voices, those ghostly voices I'm pretending are part of the history of Ireland: great sailors come ashore, feral children digging for peat to warm their families, James Joyce looking out toward a lighthouse imagining the vile erotic verbiage he'll eventually pen to his wife, Nora. My head yearns for company.

In the morning, I feel the slough in my mouth. I wipe my teeth with my T-shirt. I look at the road below me and notice all the cow patties that surround me like small, dirty brushstrokes in the grass. I imagine finding the Cliffs of Moher today, walking out to the end of the world and looking down at the sea seven hundred feet below, all the seagulls soaring cliffside, hovering, and then jumping to my end. Not that I want to end it all, I don't. The romantic gesture tickles at me, though: something bold, something definitive and memorable, a story.

I start to walk, and a car coming from the direction I'm walking stops and asks me if I'm okay. I'm okay. He asks me if I need a ride to Dublin, and I tell him I've just come from there but that I'm not going anywhere in particular. In truth, I don't know where to go. In truth, I have nowhere to go. I get into his car. He's pleasant, and he holds no serial killer energy that would have the back of my neck hairs standing up. I have nowhere to go, so the conversation might be what I need today. He looks forward as he drives, as is appropriate.

We talk pleasantly but of nothing to note, except that he speaks of plumbing as if he's discovered it. He prefers certain pipes over others, "which is fact," and he prefers to be paid in a timely fashion, which I agree is only fair. He drops me off on a cobblestone street in the center of Dublin.

I walk toward a B&B sign that looks dilapidated enough for me to afford and knock on the door. A woman, who is the same width from her shoulders to the bottom of her waist, lets me in. Her hair is in a braid, and she speaks with a stutter. She asks me if I would like some coffee and coffee is the thing I want most here in Ireland. It's the thick, soupy caffeine that drains from a narrow spout of a silver kettle that allures me. She comes back from the kitchen with that same kettle and as she tilts it, she holds the lid with the pad of her middle finger. Her pinky dances as she pours. The first sip is dirty, and I can feel the coffee granules in my mouth. This is the way I like it and I thank her for the gesture.

Two nights: thirty-four pounds, including breakfast. I put my backpack in my room. I'm shaking now from the caffeine. I'll walk the streets, and look for a priest, I guess.

I end up in a train station. I have forty pounds left. There is nowhere to get money. It seems that the banks are closed all the time. Everyone stops drinking at 9:00 p.m. Americans get hungry at 1:00 p.m. right when everything has shut down for the afternoon. There's a slight disconnect here between us and them and it has to do with habit.

I see a photo booth with the curtain open. I twist the spooling stool and check its height with the line on the mirror opposite that's crossing my eyes like a Julian Schnabel painting that won't yet be painted until much later. I feed coins to the booth. I wait. There is an initial pop and flash that startles me. I wait for the next three and slowly learn that there are about five seconds between each one. Every time I start over, I am startled by the first flash. I'm in there for what feels like months. I have run out of money and am holding fifteen strips of four photos: laughing uproariously; curiously look-ing off to the side; surprised at someone who's just arrived; reading a newspaper I've found on the ground, the middle torn out so the camera could see my face; and all the scary faces I could come up with, which were only variations on the same three or four. Sixty photos of me: my story, the one I'm going to tell people then, maybe, show the photos.

I pull open the curtain, and there is a little girl and her mother waiting to use the booth. I don't know how long they've been standing there but it feels like a long time. This is Irish patience. This is Euro-pean patience. I look down and smile and move to my right, and the little girl runs to the spool seat, which is far too high for her to sit on.

The bank is still closed when I walk over to it, and I come back and tell the gentleman in the booth in front of the theater with a stoicism I have never felt that I would be back with his money. I wasn't sure when, but I would, indeed, return it at some point. "What a movie, huh?" he replied, and I nodded and walked away with the proud stride of an Arabian horse.

Christy Brown painted with his left foot. Under the spell of his cerebral palsy, he was able to control only his left foot enough to express a talent his whole body and spirit housed. His determination was superhuman, and the stubbornness with which he conducted his life was nothing short of functional rage. I understood that functional rage. It had paralyzed me. Yet, with Christy, it had driven him. I walked along the River Liffey while I thought about my fear. I walked until it was night.

The next morning, I awake in my malnourished, too-narrow bed, but it is nice to wake up inside. I'm not sure how much talent I have. It's time to find a priest. I must become a priest. I put on my shoes and leave the room. As I start to descend the stairs, I realize I haven't put pants on. I turn around, hoping nobody comes out of their door on the second floor. The floorboards creak. My door is unlocked and has a small knob. I go back inside, and I sit back down on the edge of the bed. What is the matter with me, I think to myself. I am no Christy Brown, I say to myself. I put on my pants. I try again.

I walk to a church. I've seen the steeple before from afar. The front door is locked. I knock. I knock again and wait. It unlocks and opens. It is dark inside and I don't see anyone right away, just the colors of stained glass swathed on pews, then a man with a robe tells me that there isn't a Mass for a couple of days. I tell him I need to speak with him, and that I'm an actor who needs the help of a priest. He opens the door and asks for me to come in.

2021

DIVORCES HAVE COME AND GONE yet the heart still grows, and spring is here. The garage smells of gasoline after the motorcycle ride I took yesterday to the coffee shop, and the man with the beard and Covid mask hanging off the side of his face burped as he passed me, and yet spring still sings and is here! The women are all meditating braless before they go out into the blossoming streets smiling and maybe frowning, imagining things that may or may not be true, yet spring is here, yes, spring is here. And mentors yell at students pretending to know what they know because we all know that secrets are sharp and nobody's wisdom is sacrosanct and spring is revealing itself and bigger than you and me, yes, bigger. Spring, she is here. And, always, the children raised and the children that are being raised are frolicking together outside this pink house while what looks like cotton balls are drifting downward from the sky and, yes, oh yes, spring is here! I am lying down on the sidewalk with spring, and with the heat and spring, she falls lightly on me and the status quo factory sometimes confuses, and spring is here surrounding me with color and this strange strange banter with so-called humanity who tick and tweak and sometimes treat it all like it's never going away is lessening. But spring, I tell you. Spring! Long after you and me. Spring, for the taking.

2003

I WENT DOWN TO THE PIAZZA EVERY MORNING before most people woke up. She had long brown hair, and always took her time taking my order. She wasn't Russian beautiful, but she was beautiful in the way that you knew she could handle anything that came her way: kids, your stupidity, money or no money. She exuded that kind of resilience and wherewithal. It was in the way she walked. It's how she made me work for any eye contact at all. *"Uno cappuccino, per favore."* She looked me over like I was dim, like I was less than a number. It worked. I'd attached some romance to her that morphed her behavior from an insult to a hazing. She disappeared before I could say anything, and I was left with the trickling of the Medici fountain on the edge of the square, the pigeons cooing, and the old lady who shuffled by without even a look. But I was home, it felt. The day before I had walked along the parameter of a vineyard just outside of town. Dogs barked at me as I passed homes that have been there for centuries. Rabbits hopped across my path. Life is more alive there: smoky wine, emotional conversation, long volleying dinners, and the end-of-the-night walk through the village to help the digestion.

I felt her near again and the cappuccino landed in front of me on the round plastic table. I looked up and she'd already vanished. I imagined us in a home together. There were kids running around, a lot of them. They all had dark hair. I saw her out in the front yard with the valley beyond her, full of cypress and olive trees. I heard inside my ears a violin being played by a young boy. I took a sip of the cappuccino. It was maybe the best I'd ever had—thick and made with scorn but still suggestive.

Now, she's there again, at the table, and stares at me. I wait for her to scream. But instead she stands there as if bored with my immovability. She sets down a biscotti on the table. I didn't ask for one. She sets it on its own small white plate. She stares at me like I might be there one day, but for now I'm not. I look at the biscotti, then back at her looking at, I think, me.

1973

WHY DO WE HAVE TO LEAVE? I can't see because of the hair in my face. Mom says she likes it long. There's a wolf walking across the road. It was in the road, under that streetlamp. It had long legs and a long snout. It just looked at us and kept walking. Look! Look at the tree! Someone's hair is hanging from that tree at the end of every branch. It looks like rough hair, thick spiderwebs, a blanket torn to shreds by something angry. I feel someone's eyes on me. Something is watching us. Don't slow down! Why are you slowing down?! I smell gasoline. I smell oil. I smell my mother's "face," all that makeup she puts on in the morning. It's a powdery smell, stale. It smells old. And I see her hands, the skin draped over each thin bone wrapped around the steering wheel like a dark, wet paper towel with long white nails at the end; a "French manicure" she calls it. I see the smoke of her cigarette crawling across the lining of the roof of our car. It slowly churns along above me. Maybe the car will light on fire. Maybe we'll all burn up and we'll end up in a creek somewhere with that tree hair all over us, hidden forever. Why isn't anybody talking? My brother is asleep next to me in the back all curled up like after an accident. He looks like something you'd see in a newspaper. He never looks well. He's always struggling in some way. I stare at him for a moment and watch his lips curl into his mouth when he inhales then flap forward when he lets it out. His is a labored life. I want to save him. I want to put him on the back of my bicycle and ride down the street away from here. I look out the back window and remember we aren't here anymore. I don't know where we are, but we aren't here. We are moving, they said. Well, yeah, we're moving all the time. My mom needs to move all the time. She can't stand still. They said they sold our house though. But what about Charlie, the pony? What about the dishes that you broke and glued back together, are they coming with us? What about the wall we watch *The Hunchback of Notre Dame* against every year? Where are we going to watch that now? The car continues slowly moving forward away from the life I've known and I feel and hear small rocks being crushed underneath us. It's a dirt road, then we cross a small bridge with a grave, hollow moan. I look to the door handle and think about jumping. I could run in any direction until I disappear. My dad's big though. He could catch me. My mom would be yelling at him for years to catch me. "CATCH HIM," she would yell in the biggest letters. Maybe he wouldn't. Maybe he doesn't care enough. I feel eyes on me, but not from those in the car. They never look at me. I might be gone already. They wouldn't know. "Mom." "What?" And we all go silent again. There's eight of us in this car: my mother, father, brother, two dogs, a cat, a small cougar in a cage, and me. But nobody is making any noise. It's like it's so late time fell off somewhere. Time is dead at the bottom of a cliff sucked out of the window of the car and suffocated from the smoke that's rolling along the ceiling. Or it looked at the door handle and opened it so fast we didn't hear it. Time is running through a field somewhere. Small little imperceptible time, huffing and puffing, looking to get away fast. I look out the window deeply into the dark and think that maybe I see her. Time, running away, faster than I could ever catch her.

1999–2000

MY GIRLFRIEND WAS GETTING MINOR SURGERY. I had my eleven-year-old and my seven-year-old with me. We were visiting her in England. She kept pushing that we should travel, so we eventually came up with Scotland. I'd always had a thing for Ireland, but Scotland never really came up before then.

The Isle of Skye is a paradise. I would learn later that most of our ancestry comes from the Highlands of the Isle of Skye: Clan Ross and Clan Reed. Maybe that would explain the feeling we had when we were there. The kids and I had a banter: "Where are we going to sleep tonight?!" I'd yell, to which they'd reply in equal decibels, "We don't care!" We didn't care. We were carefree and happy. We were Clan Brolin. We were a unit.

One day about five days into a very nomadic vacation, we came across The Quiraing, a landslip on the northernmost part of Trotternish, Isle of Skye, Scotland. There was no car park at that time but for a little soggy dirt lot along the edge of the road. Everything was new to us there. Everything was a discovery. Clan Brolin just rolling along with whatever came along.

A trail was barely visible in the distance, and from it overlooked a stunning portrait of the valley below. We decided to trek and make use of our whimsy.

No water bottle. No idea how long it was, we took off: Eden

my seven-year-old holding my hand and Trevor bringing up the rear.

The walk was precarious at times. Right from the trail's edge shot down hundreds of feet, it seemed in moments. I questioned myself and my abilities as a parent. What am I doing up here? Why do I do this with little kids? What about a typical playground? Why don't you do what is already set up for children?

The trail would even out with the pitch of landscape and we'd be back to freely being our lively selves.

Sheep are in high population in Scotland. They are everywhere, and here was no exception. Blue dots on white riddled parts of the mountainside, red dots on others. I surmised the colors sprayed onto their thick wool represented ownership: Farmer Blue and Farmer Red. Fine. I like sheep. So do my kids. We've had sheep. They are funny, cartoon funny.

"BAAAAAHHHHHH!!!"

I suddenly ran toward a flock of them, my arms flailing. I thought it'd make my kids chuckle, watching them run down a hill then up another. The sheep were scared but no harm, no foul.

My children laughed more at me than at them. Our papa's crazy, and I loved living up to the legend I imagined myself to be in their minds. We love Crazy Papa.

As I stopped running and waving my hands and just started to turn around toward my kids, I heard a snap. I didn't know what it was. Then as I refocused on the herd beyond, now running up a hillside, there was one whose legs were dragging behind it, the front paws desperately scooting the body forward in fits and starts.

"Poppy? What happened to that one?"

I jogged down to where the flock had been and the lamb was still there, struggling frenetically. The closer I got the more it tried to scamper away. But it couldn't. Something wasn't working in its body. I hoped it was in shock because of the sudden change in pitch. I hoped that maybe the sheep's body had temporarily spasmed and frozen.

I put one hand on the back of its neck to try to calm it and the other I slowly pulled down the length of its spine. Vertebra. Vertebra. Vertebra. Vertebra. The sheep let out a yell. It was a screech of pain. We were two miles away from the car. That part of its back had collapsed. It moved. Something is broken.

I've been raised with wild animals my whole life. Bobcats bit my cheek until it bled, and I've cleaned the cages of wolves, mountain lions, and bobcats since I can remember. I know how to deal with crisis. I would've been a good soldier. I am calm under copious amounts of stress.

I looked over my shoulder to my kids. They were staring at me, waiting for a sign of how to react.

"Stay there," I told them.

Please, stay there. I don't know what to do. I was kidding. I was making a joke. This goddamn sheep's back broke. How the fuck did that happen?! It was only meant as a joke. What do I do?

But I kept the face on.

I looked around for anyone else on the trail. Nobody. I looked up to the peaks of The Quiraing, how the fog was just caressing the tips of them, and I suddenly felt the cold front of death enter my body.

The sheep scooted slightly farther forward and bleated.

I grabbed its body and attempted to swing it onto my shoulders. I couldn't. It was too heavy. I wanted to be that parent who could lift cars to save their child, but no matter how I tried to hoist it, I failed.

I looked back to my kids, who looked sad and anxious but stoic. They had in them that ranch kid grit that didn't allow for an instant reaction. They knew it was going to get worse and to react now would be premature.

"Turn your heads."

They did.

I could break its neck, I thought to myself—one startling snap and it would be out of its misery and pain. What if I waited, would it be better? Where is everyone?!

I avoided it as long as I could. The sun was getting lower in the sky and all I knew was that I was going to have to kill this innocent animal.

I grabbed its muzzle with my left hand, then brought my right hand over the left side of his head, leveraging my left. I'm going to pull as hard and as fast and I can and it'll go out like a light. One. Two. "Turn your heads. Cover your ears." They did.

One. Two. THREE. I pulled as every organ in my body fell into this hell of my own making.

"BAAAAAAAEEEEEEEEE!!!"

The screaming. The sheep kept screaming. Its back legs were splayed out and it just screamed and screamed as it kept reaching forward away from me. It knew. It knew I was here to murder it.

There was no sign of physical trauma. None.

"Can we look?" my son yelled over his shoulder.

"Not yet."

I didn't know what to do. My kids were watching me. This was a seminal moment. There was no pride in trying to kill the sheep. There was nothing but shame and inadequacy. I didn't know what I was doing. I should know. I was thirty-one years old. I grew up on a ranch. I grew up around wild animals. I had to assist in the deaths of animals all the time in our house: cancer, age, trauma.

I wrapped my hand around the nape of its neck. I told it I was sorry. I was sorry. I didn't know what to do. I had killed wounded animals before: a stork on a beach with a broken neck, birds flying into windows who could never fly away again; I put my dog down when he was riddled with cancer. I should know how to do this.

We were fifty feet from the edge of the cliff. I could throw it off, but what if it survived? I don't know what's down there. What if there's hay or a soft bog?

I looked up and the other sheep were watching me from afar.

My daughter was crying by now. It was a soft cry, a silent cry, just tears. My son put his arm around her. Ranch kids consoling each other through each of nature's traumas.

But this was because of me. Do they think, if I kill this sheep, that I would kill them? Not now, but at any point in their lives? If I do this will it always be living somewhere under their skin, itching at them?

I dragged the sheep up the hill while it continued to bleat and try and hold its ground with its front hooves.

There was a loose rock. It was an old rock with a layer of mica and a slight fur of moss covering it. I picked it up and there were two sharp edges visible. I ran my hand over them. They were as sharp as they looked. I imagined the sheep telling me to put it out of its misery, but I knew that wasn't the case. It had no say in the matter. It was all in my head. The truth is we were all dying on that landslip but soon one of us would be dead.

My aim. My aim had to be right on.

"Turn your heads. Cover your ears."

My daughter wiped away the tears on her face with the backside of her right hand, then put the palms of her hands over her ears. My son followed suit.

I lifted the rock above my head. One eye stared up at me from near my feet. The grass along the trail was a deep green. I imagined blood on it. I tried to prepare myself. I am a killer. I kill innocent beings. I'm not funny. There is nothing funny about me. Don't think. Aim. Save this animal from the pain I caused it. Aim! Please, God. Please let me get it right. I stand tall, the rock suspended above me.

Thunk.

A dull sound.

It's moving.

Please, God.

"Keep your heads turned."

Small bursts of wind came.

Lift.
Thunk!
Lift.
Thunk!
Lift.
Crack.

Silence.

the wind is picking up.
my children are cold.
i am cold.
the world is cold.
i feel my children inside me.
i see their pain through me.
i feel for the pulse of the animal.
silence, except for the winds.

none of us move.
i am looking down.

my children are looking away.
the sheep is dead.

we stand for a long long time.

we stand there to this day.

1992

IT'S ON A WALL SOMEWHERE in some stranger's house, probably picked up years ago at a flea market. You took a photo of me on my motorcycle, through a car window with your friend, another monsoon of a woman, then gave it to me framed as a gift, and I let it go in a rage; I threw it in the garbage bin out back. The next day it was gone, a lost symbol of unadulterated youth and sensuality.

We ended up in that dilapidated motel room dead in the fire of day, all turquoise green and hotheaded orange, when I leaned back, naked, in that sallow plastic bathtub against a leftover razor, slid down, and it took a gum-stick-thick slice off my right shoulder. I didn't feel the sting right away, but I saw in the water the swirl of a cloudy red, a blood dance.

And you sat next to me in that tub, straddling the toilet, with your brow furrowed, looking down toward my feet. That was the staple look back then of an artist in the making, that era when the desert wind was the perpetual furnace that heated our overactive sense of unique and chaos; and as tortured as we were then, later is always a sadder story. We lived, for sure, but there was no way of knowing I would outlast you. There was no way of knowing that. The look you gave me from that toilet was one of mourning; it was sure you knew I would live a short life, a tragic life, when it turned out that it was you who would die younger than what was your right.

We had our time though, you and me, in wayward motel rooms and on long Harley-Davidson pulls melting along in that age-old desert heat, avoiding anxious coyotes along the road, and passing stoic hawks on fence posts at ninety miles per hour in the sexy blur of a brushstroke.

I'll miss you.

2006

THE EL CAMINO MOTEL. I don't remember what the room number is but they're all the same: Room 8 looks like Room 12 looks like Room 6—a queen bed, pulsing plastic alarm clock, beige carpet, paper-thin Sheetrock, a sliding aluminum and glass door to the shower bath, small knobs on a small sink on either side of a small spigot. My hat sits on a cheap wooden chair and my blue jeans seem foreign against the dirty floral print of the bed's duvet. My boots stand alone next to the door with socks draped over the tops of them, as if they belong to somebody else. A film script sits open on the small Formica table to a scene where I hitch a ride with a stranger and he gets shot by the bad guy the minute I climb in and close the truck's door with a metal-crunching slam. I don't work until it's dark tonight. Outside it's hot. It's summer. I hear high heels against concrete, and I pull back the curtain and there she is, standing in front of me at the other side of the window. I unlock the door. Let her in. She doesn't even look at me, just walks right past, wafting in a scent of plane food. She puts her bag down, walks into the bathroom, and closes the bathroom door behind her. I hear the shower turn on. My stomach cringes, contracts. I feel the heat of the day behind me, and the heat of what's to come. I wish it were nighttime already. I wish my kids were here. I wish there were some things I just didn't have to do.

1995

IT STARTED WITH CUTTING OFF MY THUMB. It was the only scene I was set to do with him. He'd grab my face, breath in sync with my panicked breaths (his idea), then walk away after he'd handcuffed my wrist to an immovable object (a pipe, I think it was). That's when I'd cut my thumb off in a desperate move of panic. Years ago, I remember seeing Nick Nolte sitting at a café as I raged down Columbus Avenue after a fight with my then wife. Our eyes met in what seemed like the future gazing for me. Now, years later, there we were, both present, staring at one another, breathing. I looked into his eyes, and I didn't see Nick at all. I saw only the man he was playing, the character. This was big boy school: real actors, crazy people.

I was lucky to have this film, as it was coming out of a run with Miramax that started with *Flirting with Disaster*. That was a film Miramax actively didn't want me for. I was a loser. I was someone who had never hit but was supposed to have. I'd had *The Goonies* but that was long over and I had done nothing of note since. I was past the point of rediscovery. But David O. Russell, the director, fought for me. I was this guy in his mind, and even though it was only his second film, he fought tooth and nail for my inclusion. Miramax acquiesced but in reaction gave me nothing: no money, no credit, no love. It didn't matter. I was used to it and I was happy to be there.

This was after that.

This was after they liked me, believed in me. In essence: I was one of their "new guys."

I looked in his eyes and was scared. This was a real actor. It was this type of actor that I aspired to be. I wanted to lose myself in roles. I wanted people to be scared and unsure about what I'd do next. He's dangerous, I'd hear them say in my mind. I accepted future awards in the present. I demurred and lifted my arm up grasping gold.

He walked away—Nick: the great Nick Nolte—and I screamed the loudest, murderous scream I could conjure. I looked at my arrested hand, trying to stay in whatever state I thought someone whose death was imminent would be in. I was both objective and subjective in a moment. I was hoping that I was becoming a real actor.

CUT! Great. That was great. We got it.

I looked over at the director, a man from Denmark who didn't know yet that nobody would ultimately see this film. But he knew what was coming from me. He knew I wanted to be the best I could be with the great Nick Nolte.

I'd like to do it once more. I have an idea.

We have it though. That was great. You were great.

But I'd like to do one more thing, if it's all right with you?

He sighed. He looked down. The crew waited for his answer.

Twenty-seven years old and a periodic drug addict, half of my childhood friends dead from the throes of what our Cito Rats crew became. But I was over here making it in Hollywood. I was a success story. I was different than dead. I was breathing with Nick Nolte.

Nobody could take away that I was giving it my all. I could see that some people thought I was crazy. They liked that sort of thing then, though. It fed into a mythology that was still celebrated at that time. Nick was one of the princes of cultivating that level of mythological status. One more take. Go further. I have an idea.

Okay. One more.

After action was called, Nick strolled in as his character, said the few ominous words of dialogue that were required, breathed with me, then left. I screamed again. Grabbed a knife. Cut my thumb off. Pulled my hand through the cuff. Hyperventilated. Shock. Fear. Relief. This is going really well. I've transformed into the character. I feel this. I'm being dictated to by something I can't quite put my finger on.

I opened my tear-laden eyes. I was tingling. I was lying in a shadow on the ground. I looked up to a cameraman looking at me curiously and confused. I realized I'd passed out. I'd lost consciousness.

CUT! Check his head.

What's wrong with my head?

You landed on your head. You have a huge goose egg.

How?

We have it.

How did I fall?

I don't know. We have to move on.

Okay. Sorry.

All those years back the great Nick Nolte had locked eyes with me on a street in New York City and recognized an earlier self in my mind. I told him the story later and he responded with a smile and a nod, which I've now learned, from listening to most twenty-seven-year-old actors myself, is like the characters in Charlie Brown listening to their teacher: muffled gobbledygook.

Nick saved my life later that year. I was creating a character to live in at all times for this film, and that character was so self-destructive the human Nick Nolte felt compelled to help. We both fluctuated through the years in our friendship and in our self-destructive manifestations.

But Nick Nolte was going to kill me, then he ended up saving my life.

2022

I AM GRATEFUL for the two-inch-by-three-inch portrait of my mother as a sixteen-year-old that rests on my desk. It reminds me to honor all the cremated animals from our past burned and dusted inside the wooden urns on the bookshelves to my right, the most important holding my mother herself. She shares hers with Reggie, the chimp she spent most of the last seven years of her life with.

And I am grateful for the rain outside, its constancy, and for walking down along the creek that is too overflowing to cross with any truck, so we're stuck here, on our ranch, happily. Our little angel daughter climbs up her first John Deere dozer in the shed and makes vroom vroom noises as she pretends to work the gears and steer its wheel while I watch my wife swing on the tire hanging from the tree that monkey used to hang off and hoot from thirty years ago. I am grateful for the call with my son last night as he excitedly gets lost in the hills of New Mexico and I am grateful for FaceTiming with my older daughter, who plows a trail with her dog and fiancé through the northeastern snow. I'm grateful that everyone seems to be exactly where they're supposed to be, even my mother on the desk here at the house.

I am grateful that this is the only place I've ever loved to live because I've been emotionally tilled into its dirt. I know the back roads and I've walked and ridden them all on horseback and on motorcycles drunk and sober, both in pain and with joy.

And I'm grateful I know, being from here, what it feels like to pull a newborn from a foaling mare, and to have known the wolves and coyotes of my youth who kept me company when I was too young to know that they shouldn't have as I quietly sat with them because what else was going to happen with a mother who only trusted those animals to instill in us something useful for my brother and me. We were merely human and she didn't have much use for mere humans in her lifetime.

It's not something that's ever deconstruct-able until later when I take the time to think back on it with images of that maternal moon that has soothed me on so many despondent nights or when old ranchers who would come to visit with their fat-faced Chevy trucks and gawk when they'd see a mountain lion chasing a small boy, who was my brother, across our dirt road. He never understood not to run away. He never got that. Maybe I never did either.

1993

MOST PEOPLE ARE SITTING ON THE SUBWAY as it bangs around, but my son and I are standing. It is rush hour and we are in the middle of it.

My son is younger than five, and he's holding on to the stainless steel vertical pipe that's bouncing up and down like an epileptic pogo stick. Everybody on the train is quiet but the snap and screech of steel reverberates. I notice how people have somehow incorporated an ease into their natural algorithms: some read papers, others just stare at the person across from them without any expression, and most listen to music on their portable CD or cassette players.

There's a tap on my leg, and I look down to find him staring into my eyes, looking like he wants to say something but obviously not knowing how to say it. I crouch down and hold on to the pipe for support. "What's up?" He looks down toward the other end of the car. I follow his gaze only to find a panoply of people minding their own business. I immediately imagine he's seeing a crisis: a foaming at the mouth, choking, a water breaking, a small child being slapped. "What? What are you looking at?" "The guy," he replies. "Who?" "The GUY. Him. There. He doesn't have leg." I scan the car and find the guy with no leg. He's a pleasant-looking fella with curly, dirty blond hair. One pant leg is full, while the other just hangs there like a brown newspaper draped over the gray bench seat. I feel the man notice us (though without looking over) talking about him. I'm sure it happens all the time: covert gawking at the guy with no leg. "What do you think happened to him?" Trevor whispered. "Why don't you go ask him?" Trevor looks at me as if I just told him to go shit in somebody's mouth. He was a shy kid, but his curiosities always got the better of him. "Should I?" "Yes, you should. You want to know, right?" He nodded his head. "Then go ask him. I'm sure he'd love to tell you."

When Trevor gets nervous, he always resorts to formal. His walk becomes stiffer, his torso is lifted, and his head stays perfectly still. As he paces over to the man with no leg, he never looks back at me, as you think most kids of that age would.

The man with the curly hair looks at him as he approaches, listens to him, looks to me, then looks back to the still under-five-year-old boy. You never know what's going to happen in a situation like this. This guy could get insulted, get up, and go nuts: scream, yell. The ambiance here is thick with overt fallibility.

I watch them closely, just to make sure, at the ready. I can hear nothing of what is said, then, just as nonchalantly as when he had tapped my leg, my little boy turns around and walks right back to just where he had been a moment before, next to and under me. I look down and he is staring off in the distance like most everyone else on the train. I look to the guy without a leg, and he smiles at me, which I take as a gesture of respect: You're raising a good kid, man. Good on you, I hear a voice I've made up say in my mind.

I tap Trevor on his shoulder. "What did he say?" Trevor looks like a man now, like something in him has transformed since the short conversation he's just had with the man with no leg. His eyes are different: mostly patient. "Can you hear me? What did he say?"

1977

MY BROTHER AND I SLEEP IN TWO TWIN BEDS; both have slaughterhouse-red duvets. My mother calls them "the little brick beds." She comes in drunk some nights, sits on the edges of those big bricks, and asks us what she did the night before, and why everybody's mad at her. Sometimes we tell her. Sometimes we don't.

Each morning I walk up to the fence. I open the gate to the horse corral and walk in. One of them inevitably comes forward. There she is, a mare, carefully nuzzling my hand. Her whiskers. She pulls her lip back, and a veil of black soot is exposed on the upper gumline of her mouth. I hold her neck. I feel her breath, her hard exhales stroke my face. I'm a child, slightly scared of these intimate moments, but I don't want to be anywhere other than here. I know not to walk behind her, so I touch her hindquarters to let her know I'm there. She's so sturdy. She doesn't even have to move for me to see the muscles rippling under the thin, taut red of her skin. I grab her mane and hoist myself on top of her back. She looks at me but without moving. I wonder if she'll take off running. I wonder if she'll try and show me that I should never have mounted her in the first place. I wonder if she knows what I'm thinking. I'm here to get out of the bedroom. I'm here to avoid these questions that never stop coming.

I give her a little tap with both of my heels, and she paces forward, slowly. Her power is monumental. She feels like the tractor we ride with Danny's granddaddy early on Saturday mornings at the dump yard where he works.

We ride until there are fences we can't go beyond.

My parents are like horses that maybe fell out of a trailer along a stretch of highway on the grapevine and now have gone sour. My parents have a look in their eyes that always suggests that they may bite you at some point: one has a maniacal look ready to strike at any moment, and the other has the same placid slow-stare as Lennie in *Of Mice and Men*. Both are dangerous.

I've heard it said that a horse, if it hasn't soured, is a mirror of the trust you have in yourself. Parents aren't like that, really. They're a different set of rules you have to live by.

1992

EVERY DAY SHE WORE DIRTY WHITE—an off-white blouse—and the heat coming in an open window from the typically humid summer afternoon would find it translucent. He wouldn't focus on her pants or her shoes, but the pants, he thought, were the type of polyester where the butt is embraced sternly by the fabric in a perpetual squeeze like in those old *Life* magazine advertisements in the 1970s.

He had a young boy at home, and a sex-obsessed wife. He'd write long letters on postcards to them, twelve-to-sixteen postcards long, that they would have to piece together after they had all arrived at different times out of sequence. Email didn't exist yet. Cell phones were as heavy as bricks.

He mostly spent his time alone but would sometimes venture into the night, hoping to meet someone along the way. He was shy and most of his energy went into imagining the way things should transpire in a life.

One night while he was there he passed a small café deep into an alleyway he had never been down before. His head hung down as he walked. The dog shit on the streets assaulted his nostrils, and the scent of unwashed men clouded his imagination. Then, suddenly, as hissing sounds from a steaming espresso machine gave room to romance, he was caressed by the scent of her perfume—

dazed by it—which made his feet stop. He turned to see her, nuzzled deep in a corner of the café, white with a thin dress, hair up in a bun, eyes focused on something that lay on the table before her. He walked in and sat as close to her as he could find an open seat.

There was a lot of "as if" living back then if without some drink; an aspiring writer who didn't understand words yet and only fucked older women because he knew they'd welcome it, like a snapping turtle does a sprig of lettuce. He preferred walking in the dark and passing under the occasional neon that warmed his head. The smell of the streets rose from below his feet of day-old beer and urine from the lively urethras of the slaphappy, highly sexed dilettantes. And it sat in the nostrils and lungs like a hope of what the night might have brought them, but not him. He just wanted to be involved, somehow. He wanted his body to live in several places at once, to be in all the jars being shaken. He wanted to be publicly quartered and remembered like a proper adolescent romantic. He wanted love without ever having looked into a woman's eyes who looked back at him with the same quixotic yearning.

The woman in white sat there, sipping at her coffee while he started to write on that crude paper. The relationship between pen and paper sprung passion as it whirled, describing the wisps of her hair.

He was too reticent to think what might be awaiting him if he were to step up and tell her that she was beautiful and that he did not know what to do with such beauty. That was too much for him to bear.

Later that night he walked away, solemnly leaving his love behind. He opened the thin door of his flat and closed it softly behind him without noise. He reached up and turned on the small TV, and as the image slowly cured onto the screen, he laid back on his bed, adjusted his pillow, and listened to the weary French-speak that he was so far away from getting his head around. The scent of the woman in the café lingered and the great romance with her left in a journal on pages scribbled and warm gnawed at him in little whispers. He laid his head back against the wall and watched the black-and-white images on the TV as they came in and out of clarity until, finally, he fell off to sleep.

In class the next day, he thought he should know the teacher's name, the French woman in her fifties who was doing her best to instill in her students an understanding of how important the French language was. The way she teed off a vowel and how it would easily roll along the pink of her mouth until the vowel landed in its proper place. He watched her, but he never really listened to what she was saying. There were other people in the room, but not as far as he was concerned.

In a moment, the teacher looked to him and asked him a question in French. He became nervous and felt the heat of his voice stuck inside his throat. He looked down while she walked up to him and grabbed his hand. He was startled by her touch. His hand in hers continued to move and he extended his arm. Under her dress it went, and the wet of her flesh spoke to him. He looked up to her unsure as to what she might be asking of him. She looked into his eyes and pulled him to stand, and mischief controlled the room. The rest of the class stood too and in single file walked out of the classroom, the last person out shutting the door behind them.

She brought him over to the desk and turned to face him. He felt relaxed now, and able to investigate the light green of her eyes. She told him to sit down on the desk, and he did. He felt himself now, as she straddled his bent, dangling legs. He felt a confidence he had never felt on top of a world that was now his to do with what he had been too afraid to take hold of before then.

The ink was slow to dry in his mind, and the words that he caressed fell onto the pages where his life was spent in a better bubble.

1982

ROCKY GALENTI'S IT WAS CALLED: a raucous Italian restaurant that was more about the presentation of an open kitchen than about the delectability of the food. It was a burning Bikram-like theatrical Italian joint in Santa Barbara, California: a succulent sauna perspiring with competitive boners that were our engines, while our little egos billowed into the great storms of laughter and taunting that reverberated through the little haunt on lower State Street until late into the early morning hours. It was a place to be your most adolescent self and, to this day, reminds me of that invincible mental state that perceived adulthood as something that should only be relegated to geriatrics and that without holding on to a bit of this ready-to-cum-at-any-second attitude, we were all doomed to the staring off into a darkness of dreams crushed and adventures unheeded.

At that point I was a prep cook and a sometimes sous chef: preparing a variety of salads, tossing around some chicken dishes, and standing in for the head pasta cook when he was too hungover to show. I smoked cigarettes and drank Jameson on the fly. I chopped salads with the passion of a heavy metal drummer and whisked the custard-based zabaglione dessert in a screaming, competitive frenzy as onlookers cheered us on. I cut the tip of my finger off slicing bread, and I lit my pants on fire pulling out a pack of matches that ignited the six others that bulged my left jeans pocket. None of it mattered. I had arrived and I knew what I wanted to do with my life: be a chef. During the day I was an emotionally clad punk rock surfer who listened to Journey on the sly, and had revolving girlfriends who were there one minute and then on to the next guy, which none of my friends saw anything wrong with. The Cito Rats, as we called ourselves, were my misfit hive that I was at the epicenter of: a group of neglected kids banding together in anger and in need with everything to say and nowhere to put it. In short, I wasn't looking at much of a future in anything, but this seemed to fit pretty well until jail, or a horrible accident, took me.

My fellow hornets and I spent most of our time before school, during lunch, and after school on a muddied slab called The Gate. It was on the outer edges of the huge school property housing 3,500 daily students. One day, while we were down there pissing in the bushes, smoking out of empty dented Coke cans, or running from cops, I remember the tennis coach talking to his Izod-clad protégés, pointing with his overextended arm in our direction, obnoxiously bellowing: "If you want a meaningless life, just jog over there, and that's the group for you."

There was an old man who worked at Rocky's with a white, nicely trimmed beard who sang the arias of famous operas and would sashay from table to table during his attempted high C's. His voice was powerful and welcoming, and as tips came in the form of shots and glasses of red and white wines, he tripped along, igniting those who came for the experience, if not for a decent loaf of bread and some deep-fried mozzarella. And there was the caricaturist who patrons would pay to have their visage sketched in humorous exaggerations on any empty space left on the wall, a wall already full of drunken characters more than willing to have their blackout stamped upon the place they probably wouldn't remember the next day.

It was a profitable chaos for a while, and I was there during that while. I went home with waitresses and I partied with the older cooks until some fight broke out or someone started a fire. Singed, I wanted to be there among these pirates of the culinary constituency.

"Order up!!!" How it came in shrieks again and again moved me. And over and over the pans flew and the breasts landed sizzling. "Order up!!!" The torn sheets of scribbled paper ripped off the order wheel ending up in shreds on the rubber mats below us. It didn't matter what we cooked. It didn't matter what they ate. The debauchery was in full swing: the circus was open, and the animals were being quickly led out, one by one, ready to jump on their painted circus stands and do their thing.

It was everything to me, a life with that kind of abandon. I thought it would last but it didn't. The cooks, the waitresses, the sex, the tenor, the artist, the red and green stoplight reflections off the restaurant windows, and the chaos along the longest mahogany bar in Santa Barbara along with what happened after closing time, all would lend itself to a later life I never saw coming: acting. Acting is just some tainted mirror of life in a condensed storyline form: our lusts displayed on a silver tray ready to be eaten by anyone willing to spend their last dollar on a hope of what otherwise would be another lonely night.

2006

(Summer)

I WAS STAYING IN THE EL CAMINO (sadly not there any longer, but replaced with a hipper, more disinfected motel with some other flaccid contemporary name like Inn on the Walk) and I was woken up to a phone call from my ex-wife, my son Trevor's mother.

The El Camino was a run-down motel at the end of the main drag of Las Vegas, New Mexico. We were shooting *No Country for Old Men* there, working nights mostly. I had a buddy visiting from a theater club in LA we were running together. He was staying in another room I had reserved just for him. The only other person I knew who was staying at the motel was our prop master, Keith, who I'd known for years, and our need to keep it gritty and gross and down-to-earth paralleled. Nothing went on in that motel, but an ominous feeling lived there. Whether it was a death that had happened years before or just current shenanigans didn't matter—you knew the setting defaulted to bad luck long before it did good luck.

The phone call came in a couple of hours after I had gone to sleep, just as the sun was coming up. We had worked all night—me shooting at Javier's character and he shooting at mine.

I rolled over when I heard the clanging of the rotary phone. "Hello?"

"Someone just came over. Police. They can't find Trevor."

"What does that mean?"

"A cop came over at five a.m. 'Do you know where your son is?' type of thing. He was out last night, with his friend. I called around to the hospitals. They brought in two burn victims last night. They don't know who they are. They are taking impressions of their teeth."

"And you're saying that could be Trevor?"

"I don't know."

I put down the phone and my whole body was shaking. I had no control over it. I started to slip into visions of what it was to have a son who'd passed. This can't be. Not my son. My son and I did a "happy face trek" through France, from Nantes to Dijon, when he was four years old. We laugh together. We laugh together all the time. My son loves me. What do you mean burned beyond any recognition? I know exactly what my son looks like. He's my son!

I called as many hospitals in Los Angeles as I could. They all had someone dead. Dead people kept turning up and I wanted to know if any were my son and his friend.

"Can you look? Can you find out? I can send you a picture of what he looks like."

"Hold, please."

I called another hospital.

Then another.

Then another.

Where was my son? Is he a charred body sitting there waiting for someone to remember him?

"Hold, please."

"Hold, please."

"Hold, please."

MY SON!!!!

I explained the situation to the final hospital where he might be. "Hold, please." I knew I'd be calling random hospitals after that, desperately willing my son to appear, laughing.

It was a good five minutes before someone else came on the line, and five minutes in purgatory is five long hours of something barely related to the time we've become accustomed to.

"Hello, this is Dr. ____."

"I'm looking for Trevor Brolin, my son."

"Who is this?"

"This is his father. I'm in New Mexico right now. I'm working."

"Hold, please."

This time it wasn't so long. Another doctor came on and very calmly—as if already suggesting the death of my boy—said,

"Is this Mr. Brolin?"

"Yes."

"Your son is here."

I suddenly saw the remains of my son. I saw him in a drawer, blackened, just like the first hospital had described.

"Is my son alive?"

Pause.

"Yes, he is."

"Is he maimed in any way? An accident? Is he all right?"

"He's fine."

"What does that mean?"

"He was drunk. He's sleeping it off. Alcohol poisoning."

He was the only one who had been admitted, no friend. A young night out gone too far. The son of a well-known alcoholic.

As I was talking with the doctor, little did we both know that Trevor had woken up and in true Brolin form discharged himself from the hospital by simply walking from the bed out the front door, wearing only green hospital pants: no shirt and no shoes.

He walked down Wilshire Boulevard, his shoulders exposed,

his face to the sun. He was late for work, and when he got there, he had second-degree burns.

"Sorry I'm late," Trevor lamented.

They looked at him, put their heads down, then dismissed him.

I spoke to his mother around that time. Our son was alive and hungover. Our son is growing up. Our son is playing with the fire that I lit in him.

I thought death had raped us for about forty-five minutes. Yes, raped: entered unwanted, violated, and tore up our insides. That's the way it felt. I shook uncontrollably. All self-consciousness disappeared. Family is everything. It always has lived in me as a white blood cell and protected me from all the shit of the world. As a foundational reality, my family has always been everything good. The world fluctuates randomly, not good nor bad. Nature assaults then caresses. People come and go. Life begins then it ends. But I had always thought midlife finals happen to other people. With my mother, life existed as a chaos, but with my son the pressures of being responsible for something so precious to me meant everything. Since that phone call, it landed, maybe for the first time in my life. There is no reason for my son to be here, me to be here, or anybody else, for that matter. Life hangs on the precarious silk thread of a tenuous web. We are in a marathon and that race doesn't have a foreseeable finish line.

We crossed something a while back that resembled a line when my son was sixteen, but it fortunately wasn't a finish line. I know it's there—all of ours—and it'll be undeniable when we cross it, but until then . . .

2020

AT THE PLAYGROUND TODAY a man with a small portable tape deck in his pocket walks by as I am lying with my sleeping newborn, who is all swaddled up in a fleece snowsuit. He is playing a Native American prayer we can all hear. I look up and over at him when I hear the chanting suddenly overtake the few screaming kids and far-off leashless dogs and there he is, slouched, with dirty raven hair hanging down to his belt line, shuffling by. My daughter stares at me and I stare back but keep him in my periphery. The evening drops in temperature and there's now a still chill in the air that wasn't here a few minutes ago. People are standing up from their blankets, rubbing their hands together, finishing conversations about divorce, back problems, and new healers they've come across during the summer. Every woman looks like she went through college with a softball scholarship, and every child looks like they were born by accident.

And I look to the Indian again, the chant blending into the breeze now, still hunched and shuffling, and I remember a shaman I used to know who was ninety-five and who smiled a lot with his thirty-four-year-old blond girlfriend. I would sit in a tent with him with hot rocks hissing, the lungs singeing, the head swimming, and he'd be looking at me, smiling, still smiling, all the time smiling. I'm sure he fucked that young ingenue regularly. You could tell by the way she looked at him.

People are leaving, even the shuffler whose music walks away with the wind, and my daughter still hasn't unlocked her eyes from mine. I can see the deepening chill on her face in the way she's shifted her gaze at me. I know I'll see that man again. She's still looking at me, as if she knows something that I won't find out until much later, as if the cold that came holds in it something that I'm not capable of picking up on. I envy her sensitivities, that darkest place that speaks in nothing but feelings.

1974

I AM WAKING UP. We are in a smaller motel than the one we were in two days ago, and I can hear the crunch of someone walking by outside, maybe a worker. Also, the whoosh of a car brushes past while my head presses against the wall.

They should slow down.
 I'm sure there's more children here besides us.

Light peaks through a small crack in the curtains so I know it's morning. Daddy's still asleep and so is my brother; he's on the floor with my pillow. He says he doesn't like anything soft, so he sleeps on the wood floors below me.
 Daddy says he wants me to write every morning; he says he wants me to put down what I'm thinking on a piece of paper, but he also says I can draw a picture instead if I want to.

He says he wants to know what I'm thinking more.
 He says I stare off into the distance a lot and I think he gets worried about it.
 I don't know why.

Something smells in here. Maybe it's old sweat on the mattress. I don't know how many people have slept in this bed. It's gross to think about.

Daddy and I sometimes have to share a bed, and sometimes all of us do, but my brother always, at some point, ends up on the floor. Once in a while I get my own smaller bed, and they share a small one together. It's funny because one or the other ends up falling on the floor during the night, then they get mad at each other, but I always laugh with my hand over my mouth. Nobody can see anything because it's dark.

It's morning now though, and I'm hungry. We ate at the gas station last night: burritos cooked in their microwave, three Fantas, and three packets of M&M's. We sat on the curb with paper towels on our laps and watched people outside a bar across the street called Bando's, which sounds like a clown to me. I kept expecting a clown to walk outside so I kept forgetting to eat. I don't like clowns. I like unicorns.

I wish they'd wake up, so we can go. Maybe I'll turn on the TV. I wonder if this one works? I'll turn the volume all the way down so I don't wake anyone.

2008

I WAS IN THE GREENWICH HOTEL, in the sitting room, on the opposite side of where the fireplace is. Sean Penn and I were dressed in suits and ties: his staple black suit with a starched white shirt, and mine a black on black on black. Robert De Niro came and sat in one of the plush leather chairs placed in a circle, joining our drinking bout—mine, really. I was to receive an award from the New York Film Critics Circle for my stint in the film Sean and I did together, *Milk*.

Bob sat down and we were introduced. We shook hands and he slumped back in his chair the way an owner of a hotel might: tired and with a look of having had enough of it all already. I had been given the opportunity to play with the big boys and I took it as if I'd always been there, but inside I was as scared as I'd always been. So, as the truest result of a mother with no filter, I played an angle only my mother could fully appreciate.

"You know . . . your face."

Bob looked at me with that look we've all seen in a million movies he's done, and I could see Sean roll his eyes and mumble: ". . . shut the fuck up, dude."

I continued, focusing on Bob like a great discovery: "Your face. You have a face. Anybody ever tell you that?"

"My face?"

I put up my hands outlining the shape of it and squared it off around his head. "Yeah. You ever thought of being an actor? You have the face of someone who should be seen. You ever think about getting out of the hotel business and maybe giving movies a shot?"

"What is he talking about?" Bob asked Sean, irritated.

"Nothing. Don't listen to him. He's crazy."

"You got a fucking face." And I smiled. And I was on my way.

I'd had a few glasses of wine already and I had been out the night before until morning. The wine intensified my exhaustion, and yet the alcohol always won and brought back that warrior gasoline. Be a fucking warrior, the wine whispered to me. Be the motherfucker who lays his indelible fingerprint on every person in every situation. The last thing I remember in the hotel was Bob uncomfortably trying to smile.

Sean and I took the car we were assigned to the event. I had a drink or two in the car. There was a small red carpet when we got there where a few pictures were taken: my arm heavy around Sean's shoulders; another of me yelling something at the photographer; and several of me looking behind me at something that probably wasn't there.

I talked at whomever would listen and guffawed and verbally danced, boisterous until I was asked to sit down at our assigned table. I pulled out the paper folded twice from my inside jacket pocket and reread the speech I was about to give: the speech that was in response to being honored as an actor of note. All the important writers of New York City were there and all those writers are read by every other writer in the world. That event holds the crème de la crème: the elite, the respected, the North Star of critics. I handed my written speech to my worried-looking publicist, and she read it through. When finished, she said, "You can't read that. I would not recommend it," which fed my intention more: to not succumb to the celebrity manual that highly suggested I give everyone in the room a psychic hand job. I was going to be my mother's son: a cowboy, a drunk, a rabble-rouser—my own man.

I took a large swig from my large glass of deep-red cabernet sauvignon.

Sean was asked to speak first. He sauntered up there with his usual confident gait and people looked on with respect. He was a pain in the ass, but as long as he gave great performances, his curmudgeonly ways were tolerated. He very sweetly introduced me with a grinning quip: "He goes harder than anyone I know but suffers more the next day than most."

I put my speech back in my jacket pocket and took one more swill of wine.

"Let's hear a little rant from the motormouth himself. For Best Supporting Actor: Josh Brolin."

I stood. The room acknowledged me with polite applause. I had been to London earlier in the month to receive the International Man of the Year Award. My publicist looked at me from inside that black SUV in London that we rode in, as paparazzi swarmed the red carpet, and gravely asked me if I was ready— "Yes," I acknowledged—and when we exploded from the car (that now, suddenly, felt like it was a hearse), all cameras dropped downwardly: nobody knew who I was or what I was doing there. I was not only an out-of-place Yank but I was an out-of-place Yank who was new to the scene . . . even though I'd been in this chosen profession for over twenty years doing mostly dreck and fodder. And in perfect harmony with the instant change in vibe, my publicist started to laugh.

Here was different. I was being acknowledged for something they had seen and responded to. I was there because all of *them*—a consensus, as opposed to a discovery or a publicity stunt—wanted me there. The dude from *The Goonies* had made good. I had just been the lead of a film that won Best Picture the year before, and now I was being lauded for a performance given in a film that was most likely going to be nominated for Best Picture and almost assuredly win Sean Penn the Best Actor statue.

"Thank you. Thank you, guys."

I looked out among the sea of attendees. They were smiling, proud to have given a leg up to someone who had been around relatively unnoticed for so many years. Why not, they thought to themselves. We all love success stories. We all love giving a dollar or two to some random taker: the light that comes on, the art of compassion that is reignited in welling eyes. I recognized actors I had seen and admired through the years, women who had donned covers that I had bought the magazines of and hoped to one day meet, never mind potentially work with. This was a special night. I knew that. I felt it. As I reached into the pocket of the inside of my jacket for the third time that night, I felt my head swimming and my knees shaking. Should I read the speech? I had already flipped Sean the bird in response to a cute but snide remark he had made up there from the podium. He was establishing himself. (*Fuck you. I am who I am.*) I walked up and unfolded the two letter-size pieces of paper and let it fly. (*You're not going to tell me how to be. I am dangerous. I am my own man. I'm so scared. Help me through this.*) The wine started to speak about other actors, about certain writers. Words like *motherfucker* and *piece of shit* rolled off my tongue and onto a growing din of shock and disgust. There I was on my perceived and so temporary pulpit with all eyes on me, pontificating on how I viewed *awards* and how I "didn't give a fuck about the people who doubted me or tried to erase me." The words tripped out unnaturally and I, in a flash, was inundated with images of cleaning the shit from the cages of timber wolves as a young boy. There were images from my past trying to speak to me, but I was too drunk to know of what.

Then to the silence of the room, I said thank you and walked back to my seat. A few people clapped softly. My publicist didn't and looked instead at the ground. Sean smiled a friendly smile, as your brother would while you're being wheeled back into a traumatic surgery.

I looked around knowing that I had hurt and disappointed and with a sad pride put my glass to my lips and tipped it all the way upside down, letting the flat disk of the bottom hang in the air.

Emptying.

Emptying.

Empty.

The Man on His Bum

A YOUNG BOY WAS WALKING with his father along a long of stretch of sidewalk. On their walk they passed a man sitting destitute on his bum leaning against a dilapidated wall, and in a puddle next to him, apparently, some regurgitation: a mix of what seemed like pepperoni and milk. The young boy noticed him then take off his new yellow cap that said something on the front of it and looked to the man on his bum but didn't speak to him. The man on his bum looked back at the boy and smiled softly. At that same moment, the father put a finger to his lips, telling the man on his bum that he shouldn't talk to the boy, not a word, and the man on his bum went back down to looking to the place on the ground where he had been looking before. The boy and his father walked on, and after a few steps the boy looked up and asked his father a question:

"Why is he like that?"

"Why?"

"Yeah."

"Because he wants to be like that."

"Why would be want to be like that?"

"Because he likes it outside. He likes the open air."

"That's not true. He was sick and there was sick next to him in a puddle. Nobody wants that."

The father took a moment to think about what to say, then said it.

"You might be right. I should've taken a closer look, but you don't want to think about that, do you? Come on, let's go see if we can find ourselves an ice cream or something nice like that."

"Why didn't you want him to be talking to me?"

"Because we don't know him, son. We don't talk to people we don't know."

"You say hi to people all the time you don't know. Why's he any different?"

"Come on. You know why."

The boy looked around. Up high he could see the steam coughing out of a smokestack. People walked by who he took a closer look at. He thought of his mother back home cleaning.

"Why does he scare me?"

"Because he's a scary man."

"Why?"

"Well, he hasn't washed in a long, long time, and dirty people are scary sometimes."

"I've been dirty, and you weren't scared of me."

"That's because you're my son. I'll never be scared of you, no matter what you look like."

"Then where's his father? Don't you think he needs his father now to say what you just said?"

"Sure, you're probably right."

"Why is he scary to us if he's dirty and not to his father?"

"We don't know him."

"But what if we got to know him?"

"That takes time."

"What if we had the time to get to know him?"

"Then he might be okay."

"So, what if we didn't get ice cream and get to know that guy on his bum back there, who we just passed? What if he turns out to be nice, then we could tell him what you just told me. Yeah? Maybe?"

"You're a good boy."

"Can we go back?"

The father stopped and looked down at the boy.

"We don't have time."

"Instead of the ice cream?"

"We don't have time. I have work."

The boy suddenly turned around and ran back to the man on his bum, and the father made chase but didn't get to him before the boy wrapped his arms around the man on his bum, which the man softly returned. The boy looked into the eyes of the man on his bum, and the man, like before, couldn't help but look down.

"Would you like an ice cream?" the boy asked.

But the man on his bum would not answer.

"Sir, would you like an ice cream? You better tell me now."

The boy felt a sharp pain on the back of his head. He knew his father had hit him and he deserved it by running away, but it felt worth it. He didn't know why, and he knew that it might make it all for the worse, but need was need, he thought to himself.

The three of them were frozen there on the side of the road. It was a beautiful spring day, a few bits of trash tripped along with a breeze, and people walked by, their sights rigid in front of them, maybe taking notice, maybe not.

1986

IT USUALLY STARTS SOON AFTER being away from home. The job comes and you're saturated by the mystery of it. Then you get there and it's pretty much the same: actors curious where they stand in the status of things, comparisons, lots of diversionary humor, and a few witticisms during moments of discomfort. You start thinking about home after a couple of weeks, your block, the people who nourish you with their sandpaper characters, and a culture that owns its misfits and rejoices monuments of personality: Venice-Fucking-Beach. Every morning there's that guy I pass juggling a tennis ball, a bowling ball, and a chain saw on the boardwalk off Windward Avenue as I look for a coffee handout around the front of the Sidewalk Cafe. I don't have a job. Then the inevitable pervert tries to lure me back to his apartment who I'll hit in the face then ride my skateboard down the bike path jazzed up just enough to get me through the day.

Winter brings with it the strangest light while I peer out toward the ocean at that gray-black wall invariably creeping forward, which always happens without warning, and everything sinks onto a scarier plane. Everyone who lives here knows the coming of that ominous Bermuda cloud of Venice Beach off the boardwalk when things get just a little more severe and all the tourists fly home, and the locals are left to feed off each other's ferocity. We are what the Lower East Side of New York used to be and the worst of what Florida has always been.

I will never leave here: this depth in the sewer of what will always have "original" stamped on its back-alley asshole and where there will always be, for just a buck a quarter, an oily slice of pepperoni and a medium Coke waiting for you. And as you eat it, some stray will ask you if you have a can of spray paint because he just got an idea—and I'll know I'm home: that all of the other shit is just some Nobu fantasyland smut with a thin slice of jalapeño on its sushi and a roofie waiting patiently in some yuppie's nonalcoholic beer.

2021

EVERYONE IS STILL ASLEEP, and I don't work until 6:00 p.m. I'm supposed to work all night. The kids have been sick with a horrible cough. It's desperately grabbing at me. I've staved it off so far, but I feel something that's tickling at my throat. Six o'clock is arriving too quickly.

Dune was released internationally just over two weeks ago. It looks like we'll shoot the second half of the book come June in Jordan and Budapest and, I heard, maybe far outside Abu Dhabi. After that we'll probably roll into another season of *Outer Range* in New Mexico. A couple of years of a lot of work and a couple of years of missing more of what I've become so used to thriving on—waking up every day to the trials and tribulations of being a full-time dad . . . again.

The youngest is now standing on her own. The squat-to-fully-erect lift is almost unnaturally easy for her and always performed with a proud smile as she wobbles on what seems like an imaginary tightrope. I often project the future of her life and what's to come: running with great abandon with her sister in the yard, dresses flapping in an easy wind; overconsciously waiting to be picked up from school, boys watching them as they look out for our car to round the corner; the anxiety of homework and all the sounds and grunts and attitude that come with it; the pride of graduation; first job; moving in, the words: "I love you Papa Bear" still coming from her just on the verge of adult lips. I see it all in a white flash.

This first year has gone by so quickly. That one-year-old smile permeates even the densest armor. Her heart has more capacity than I will ever possess. It's all felt in the hugs and through her eyes. Her touch, at once sensitive and wild, softens me.

Her three-year-old sister rolls an innate wonderment around the bingo basket of her mind: weighing, comparing, mathematically assessing the alchemy of it all; then she climbs it, basks in it, befriends then rejects it. She is a woman of movement.

Sister and sister. They are a powerful duo. They sing through what has become together a different instrument and it is a song beautifully attuned to what my ears prefer: a music that caresses my heart like Yo-Yo Ma's cello or Pavarotti's arias have. And with all romantic bullshit aside, it does me right, their personal ties: strong, brilliant, brave, adventurous, absurd, funny, creative, impassioned, sensitive—and those unique qualities of ownership, respect, and a lack of pandering to please others.

To be gifted with these three girls and a boy is beyond thanks. It's like a divine intervention that slapped the ego out of my self-absorbed youth. The idea touches me every couple of years of some Italian life in my seventies involving books, chess, wine, and young beautiful women slowly making the sign of the cross on themselves in front of a Medici fountain as the perspiration of an August heat wave caresses their cleavage—but then it passes.

We love. We try to.

I feed my wife with that love I feel for her, which is monumental, and our house bleeds with the knowing that we don't live by any manual dictated by anyone other than ourselves and whatever God might actually be in the making of whatever we are becoming.

So tonight, I exhale, and think back to all the bruised and dented years undenied:

I rolled cars, dove through windows, ran from cops, and fucked women I'd normally be too afraid to talk to. It was irresponsible and dangerous. I put myself in jeopardy and threw others to the wolves. I was nice, until I wasn't—"Shark eyes," my buddy T-Roll called it: "In the snap of a millisecond you went from charming to dark." The next morning I'd lie there, crawling through the black molasses of my memory and desperately searching for any evidence of what I'd done the night before. I'd wake up on the sidewalk knowing, once again, that I'd been too wet-brained to figure out how to get into my house and that I'd eventually given myself to the cold concrete of the sidewalk. But it was worth it at that point in my life. Otherwise I shook with fear. I was paralyzed with what I thought other people saw in me: a nothing, an invisible, worthless of word, and to have anything resembling character was a valued weight in this hell. I was all about me and no matter my moments of care and concern and beneficence, it all, in the end, came down to it serving me.

Now, in my fifties, I wake up knowing exactly where I am. My windows are open, which I remember opening last night. I am naked, and I remember taking off and throwing my dirty clothes in a hamper I bought the other day at the equivalent of a Hungarian Target here in Budapest. I wake up with eyes wide and I don't need coffee but I enjoy the ritual. I am right where I'm supposed to be, fully aware, and shame no longer follows me like a reticent dog being belly-dragged on a leash. With this clarity comes an interest in smiles and honest laughter and the patience to suck the nutrients from all those walks of life that now tickle my senses. Morning has me in its grip and I'll walk today, I'll stroll to the river or up the hill or to a coffee shop to witness and engage.

The world is a hard and unforgiving dark alleyway. Sometimes the riot of a bar fight becomes a communal heaven we never saw coming.

For now, I'll marvel, sufficiently stunned, at the fortune of it all.

Amen.

2002

I WENT TO PRISON IN BEAUMONT, TEXAS. I was visiting. I lied and said that I was researching a role or writing a play, I can't remember which. The truth was I just wanted to get in there and talk to the inmates and know more intimately what their experiences were and how they dealt with both confinement and their relationships with the staff.

The warden turned out to be a sober guy too and we became friendly. He granted me access that I probably wouldn't have normally been given, and staff members seemed to take a liking to me too.

Bubba, one of the guards, showed me a photo that his mother had taken during a backyard barbecue of theirs. He told his mama: "Mama, get the camera so you can get me knocking old Grayson here right on his ass," to which she replied: "Hold on. Don't do it yet. Wait!" as she ran into the house to grab her camera. The shot was midhit and the knees of the guy who was being punched were already buckling.

It was a genius photograph and the fact that it was taken by the mother at the son's request without a moment's shock or hesitation spoke volumes to me. I liked it there, but they were backwoods crazy fun. As an outsider, it was great to witness, but like Hunter S. Thompson when he was hanging with the Hells Angels—get in too deep and you may never come out.

I also saw a video of a stabbing that had happened there in the prison a few years before. They had a couple of them, but the one I'll never get out of my mind had one prisoner rushing his own cousin in a recreation cell. The victim was about to be initiated into a rival gang, and six weeks before he was to be released, his own cousin was given the job to snuff him out.

He was stabbed 132 times in the abdomen. I could see him holding his guts in. At one point he was more interested in holding his guts in than fending off the blows from the knife. What stood out was how long he stayed standing. It was minutes, not seconds.

I've been stabbed, once. To be conscious that you're very possibly going to die is a revelation. You think of the most precious things in your life all at once, all the reasons why you want to live. The romances of a special life leave you, and you are suddenly draped with a blanket of humility and with it the simplest things pull at your heart like water does for a parched dog.

Watching that video I saw the whole trajectory of that young man's life slip into death. I saw that moment when he knew that a future was no longer his to toy with. He was numb, I realized as I watched, because the pain had passed, and the simplicity of holding on to whatever slippery membranes that rendered him still human was all that presented value. I saw the sadness in his eyes. The camera was that close. The guards couldn't go in there until there were enough of them on site to protect the area, so the stabbing went on unencumbered.

I often think about how my life has had its twists and turns and I know as clear as day that there is very little separating me from what could have been that life. I hold it inside me, like that inmate was holding in his guts: just on the verge of falling out, just on the precipice of no levity at all.

2015

(Death)

HE WALKED INTO THE CHAPEL out of the dark snow. It was small and in it many candles burned softly. A painter's hue saturated the interior of it, and as he walked in holding behind him her hand, a tear fell down his cheek. It was his birthday and they were high up in the mountains of Italy in his favorite setting: a chapel.

Before he met her, she knew only his children meant anything to him. Sure, women came and went, love existed some, and then, like a quick assault or burglary, it ran away. Children can't run because they are tethered by a bloodline that is inescapable. She loved that about him. She knew that children and also their parents were, indeed, in for life, whether she liked it or not.

Birthdays represented something that he didn't like conjured but, as it happened, usually decided to surface anyway. But chapels had always brought a feeling of peace. They were personal and didn't have to exist, but did. The small societies that yearned for communal intimacy demanded it. There was no shadow at play here: the chapel brought a profound solace, as those tucked-away religious shanties represented something loftier than the pettiness people most often resorted to.

She watched him think through his reaction and she stayed close. He turned to look at her because he could feel her smile and he wanted to return it, for she stood there so proud to have put this together, just for him. It was his special day and all day she had sputtered and hiccupped through so many sharp moments of anticipation, hoping her plan would work, crunching giddily through each precarious step through the snow-carpeted forest. She led him, having walked it several times in the daylight before, counting each step aloud as she did, knowing it would be dark when the time came. He trusted her, and she felt that more than ever now. So, he followed the muted sounds of her left foot then right, and placed them softly to where hers had just landed.

The heat as they entered felt romantic. The wind blew through the trees outside and bits of snow trickled softly down off the pine needles and danced beyond the chapel windows. He sauntered past the few blood-brown pews then up to a shimmering altar where there stood a golden cross. Looking at it he remembered his mother and the night the phone rang. The anger he felt toward her leaving his life and of the many times that she had made him smile—made him cringe and ache. But after a labored reconfiguring, he would smile again.

Chapels lived in him as they lived for the people of those small towns who inhabited them, and she knew that. With each chapel they entered, knelt in, held hands together inside of, something in them grew closer toward each other.

But this chapel on his birthday, on the death day of his mother, landed in his heart and flourished, and it stayed there like that for years until his time came to leave.

Now, in that same chapel she had led him into so many years ago, she reached her warm hand down upon his cold one while the candles burned as alive as they had before, and the golden cross still shimmered stoic and dreamily where it had so long ago. She knelt down to say goodbye and put her lips softly onto his, knowing that he would've loved that it was still here, in the chapel they both loved the most, where they would spend their last moments. It was as if they were there together again for the first time: together thoroughly, happy, and for a moment without even death getting in the way.

2021

THE OVERCOOKED AND STALE GREEN-CHILI APPLE FRITTER this morning was somehow edible. I tore off pieces of it from the warmth of inside my truck with a crack and dipped it into my coffee to help these fragile getting-older teeth along. The apple came first, then the sting of chili followed. I am not home but this is a home right now. I wander.

Earlier, we were honored with prayers from some members of the Native American community of New Mexico because we start shooting soon, and that means a lot to both of our . . . parties: we stand in the dirt by a horse corral with cowboy hats at our sides and you can feel some urban still in the air, but it is dissipating, slowly melting away or hiding itself with each oncoming blessing. A humbling wind whispers against our cosmetic hardships as this New Mexican poverty that is everywhere screams at your obvious present states of affluence—as you try, as you try.

We've been waking up in the mornings to light blues and pinks on the horizon and faint wisps of snowfall, and my immediate need to walk outside to feel the cold shock on my face and listen to what the morning might have to say becomes paramount. A dip of Copenhagen tucked behind my lip gives me a small rush. I grab my rope and look upon my dummy steer as if he's already trying to get away and go on to rope his plastic horns again and again and again until my hands go numb and the pain in my fingers yearn for the heat of an overmicrowaved mug of bitter coffee.

I walked straight into the mountains yesterday as something familiar started to come back. I know this dirt. I've been here before, with other people, telling other stories, waking up in bed remembering your face, whoever you were. I'm the same ole guy, just getting older, more able to appreciate the humility of being able to be here at all, anywhere at all; I can still wake up in bed and wander through my memories before it's too late. It's what I'll miss the most when this is all over, that traveling through such memories when there's nothing but silence to take each phantom breath with, when sounds usually die as fast as they are born.

The prayers end, and the Indians walk to their respective trucks, sort of waving goodbye. We meander back to our horses pretending to know what to do.

2019

She's dreaming.
    And one day gets older,
        grows up,
            gets engaged
            on the very ranch she was raised on.

She's dreaming.
Eyes closed.
      Inside grandmother's old dress
        we wiggled her into
           who's gone now.
           Grandma.
And the little girl fills it,
a legacy,
and dreams
    and she grows,
        finding herself squeezing through the legacy
        of this family, this circus.
She gets it,
the big joke.
        Pain has come and gone
        and those adolescent demons

          that scratch

      at

         your

            psyche

            scurry

            away.

Survived. She dreams.

Eyes closed.

Wakes up.

Singing.

2009?

"MY NAME IS BARBRA," she said to me as she reached out her hand. Actually, that's a lie. I don't remember the first time we met. I'm bad like that. I don't remember the first time we met but I had heard of her from my mother years before.

"I would have liked to have met your mother. I think we would've gotten along it sounds like," she said invitingly.

"They would've loved each other!" my father exclaimed.

In fact, my mother had actually met Barbra in Sun Valley, Idaho, years before. They were both visiting Clint Eastwood, where he owned a home. My mother had known Clint and his then-wife Maggie since my mother ran away from Corpus Christi, Texas, at nineteen years old. They were the first people she met. I think it was around 1958, just before Clint had gotten *Rawhide*.

"I think you guys had met."

"No."

I remember I had seen a photo of all of them together and I remember my mother telling me that Barbra was tough.

It didn't matter. We've gone through decades spouting the good graces that could have transpired from the coming together of those two. The reality is they would've hated each other. I'm convinced of that. Tough people almost always hate other tough people unless one has let their guard down.

But I've always liked tough women. It's an Oedipal thing, I'm sure. So, the next step was to get rid of my dad.

No, I liked my dad, so that wasn't an option.

She was my pop's girl and we were all going to live happily-ever-after. That was it. That was the ticket.

Well into our happily-ever-after I walked into their house one day:

"I'll have a glass of wine," I said.

She looked at me and cocked her head, so I repeated myself.

"I'll have a glass of red wine, please."

She took a slow breath then hit me with it: "Aren't you an alcoholic?"

It was a pretty ballsy thing to say. Yeah, I knew her for a while already, she was my dad's wife now, and he was really in love with her, and from what I could tell, so was she with him. "Aren't you supposed to be not drinking?" Man, there it is again. She always had a way of washing her tongue with a bullshit cleanser before she talked with me. My own mom was like that, so it didn't paralyze me, but my own mom was dead, so this was going to have to do.

"It's fine. It's just a glass of wine," I tried to justify.

"I don't think you're supposed to drink anything, right?"

A couple of years ago she had come all the way to Prescott, Arizona, to visit me. I was landscaping at that point. I'd quit acting. Fuck acting, I had hotheadedly concluded. I had sworn off TV anyway (I hated the pace) and I was trading stocks for income, so I didn't, in case, need the acting. I was raising two kids, dealing with a ranch that had been left to me without a dime having been paid on the loan that built the house, and I was drinking.

"Hi!" She had given me a hug. I walked out of the Prescott house into the parking area and walked into the hug. Then I hugged my father.

"Why don't you tie your shoelaces?" I looked down through my long, uncombed hair. I didn't tie my shoelaces because I was still in the frame of mind that I wasn't going to do anything that was expected of me. It started with no bullshit with her and it'll end with no bullshit. It's what I've always appreciated most in anyone, no matter how much my own enemy I was.

I'd gotten sober at twenty-nine when a bunch of friends walked into the apartment I was living in on Vineland Avenue in Hollywood. The El Royale. I'd lived there for a while, and sometimes my kids were down there, sometimes they were up north, at the ranch; mostly they were with their mom. I'd tried to keep it all at bay from what meant something to me: my children. But, inevitably, those designs break because they are based on whimsy and reaction. They don't have any real foundation. So, the whole thing topples when the need is the need and the great puppet master that alcohol was for me took over.

"It's just a glass of wine. You don't have to get it, but I'll just have one later. So, why not just have it now?"

It's a puzzle, the psychology of winning, no matter the consequences. I wanted what I wanted and that was my only concern.

I'd been to jail more than a few times by then. I had put my kids in jeopardy. I had lost relationships and friendships. I knew that having a drink wouldn't make anything better but was very likely to make any situation ultimately worse.

"I'll get it myself."

"No, you shouldn't drink."

As with all in-laws, the relationship started great, soured, then grew in value. My mom was dead and nobody was going to replace my own mother, no matter how poisonous my own mother might have been.

She signed a card for me once: Love Mom. You see, there it is. Mom. You're not my mom. You're my stepmother. Who wants to be a stepmother though? Nobody. It connotes evil intentions:

drastic compensations for cosmetic insecurities; misery loves company; me me me syndrome. She wasn't that.. She wanted a family. She was being kind.

"I'm an alcoholic but I like red wine."

"You shouldn't drink."

I know.

"You know that, right?"

Yeah.

The saturating Jewish mother. I'd heard about them. I'd read about them. I'd had some friends with those. They're almost always comically on the offense.

She never saw *that* guy I was. She was never privy to those things that landed me in jail or in fights or figuring out why I was waking up on sidewalks with my T-shirt wrapped around my otherwise naked waist. That's what I understood a mom to be for the longest time. This was different. This was just plain old-fashioned mothering. I had to get used to it.

Barbra has done some great things in her lifetime. One of my mother's great stories was when she was committed to Camarillo State Hospital a couple of years after she had landed in the City of Angels. She was fucking a bunch of married men and was raised Baptist, so it was weighing on her. She decided to take too many pills one day then drive around the neighborhood. (She loved driving!)

There was a woman in that Camarillo funny farm who had chopped her whole family to pieces and hadn't spoken a word for the more than a decade she'd been there.

"I got her to talk," my mother told me after I was born.

I didn't have to ask how. I already knew. She got her to talk in the way she dealt with everything and everybody: straight down the throat.

Candy, was what the woman said.

Candy seemed appropriate for the story, true or not.

If there were more women like Jane and Barbra, would there be a lot more men like my dad?

Either way, things would be a lot more straightfuckingforward. No bobbing and weaving, just down-the-line truth without dessert.

1991

I'D HALF-CONSCIOUSLY CONSTRUCTED this part urban cowboy, part hypersexed Joycean curiositor image that my mother would have been proud of as I roamed, cowboy-hatted, week in and week out, through Père Lachaise Cemetery with baguette, soft cheese, and a few bottles of cheap red Bordeaux in hand; that is what I imagined would be my in to a society that thrived inside their respective adolescent tornados and oversexed Anaïs Nin wet dreams:

On one of those scorching dog days, I met a young woman who was even younger than I was. She was leaning against the grave of Molière, feet exposed, and hair falling softly onto her face. She summoned me by sending her girlfriend over to where I stood. I had studied the language, but the language wasn't fluent in me. I tripped through a few French sentences—something about the leaves and if she knew that Oscar Wilde was lain nearby—and soon we were in her apartment: me on top of her, her on top of me.

Sex was usually quick but kissing lasted hours in those days. As a man well into his grayer years now, my hindsight smiles at the memory of when there was no self-control, so kissing was the better alternative, especially in France, where the art of kissing and foreplay are still appreciated.

Where was that girl now? I can't help but wonder. Those scents that show up at the strangest times of old vinyls, unwashed dogs, perfume that peak the olfactory, and/or day-old cigarette smoke in a bar just about to open. All of them random but yearning for something of a more complete picture.

I'd never want to go back now though, be one of those fifty-something-year-old's trying to sage up to the young ones, desperate to be listened to, praised, and imagined great by the unshowered few. No, I'll take my memories of adventurous experiments that put me right where I am now, in the forest of my own making, and settle.

2008

IT IS QUIET THIS MORNING. It's the only time it's been quiet. Pigeons, that's all I hear. The only other thing are the tongue and groove sounds underneath the tires as they roll and skip by outside— . . . pa pap . . . pa pap . . . pa pap. I move my mouth with each one. The trees are skeletal in New York this time of year and weather predictions are about as reliable as the stock market.

It was a tough wake-up. I didn't remember again, just the dreaming. I awoke on the floor, and two girls in a bed lay above me. I walked into the bathroom and smelled myself. They weren't on me. Had we not mixed it up at all? I walked softly back into the bedroom to see if they were dead. I watched them breathe. They were fine, slightly smiling even. I gathered my clothes, drank water from the kitchen sink, looked back into the bedroom one more time just to make sure it was certain, and slipped out the door, which locked behind me automatically.

I saw a wave rise like a swelling balloon last night and felt my heart sink. There are so many things I still want to do, I thought as I rode in the taxi on a smooth road, the silence back. I wanted to look into people's eyes more than one more time. *I love you*, I thought to myself. *I love you too* followed it, quietly. Inside the dead of sleep is always the scariest place, and when you find yourself having to make a decision—scratching for safety and trying to make it to the top of Everest; turning your surfboard around and falling with every fear you've ever tried to confront down an eighty-foot mountain of water; or running from the bulls of Pamplona and you're there alone, stuck in something invisible, psychically ratcheted down—the lifesaving decision made is never the right one. That fear. That paralyzing fear. My whole life has been bullied by that fear. *I love you. I love you very much.* That fear has always tried to kill me. It haunted me. "Total commitment," I heard myself say.

The cabbie looked over his shoulder: "What was that?"

"Nothing. Sorry. Nothing," I barely said back.

I had woken up, listened to the pigeons, walked outside. There was always the next step forward to look forward to. There was always something like that probably.

2022

WE ARE TRYING TO CREATE STRONGER BOUNDARIES. She responds to that, our daughter. So does the other one, our other daughter. Today, though, at the playground, was a total freak-out and we weren't having it. She screamed in my arms all the way to the car. I was shaking by the time I closed the car door. The amount of attention she demands in a moment like that is unparalleled. I knelt down, unsure of what to do. And as I pacified her I knew whatever she was feeling would find its way out someway later.

I got back in the car while Kathryn was talking with her. I was sweating, unsure, vulnerable. It had taken two hours to get coffee this morning. I was frayed. I'm fat. I'm not a good father. All of it rushing through my head.

I suddenly got back out of the car and started walking. Home was about a mile and a half away. I was making it about me.

She pulled up beside me.

"Get in."

"No."

"Get IN."

"I can't *do* this!"

Then she drove away and at about the halfway point she showed up again, this time with a bottle of water.

"Here. At least take *this*."

"I don't want it! Can I have just a moment?! Just one?!? Leave. Just drive home. Thank you!"

I wanted the water the second she pulled away. It's so fucking humid here. The air lands on you. It doesn't just blow by like in the desert. Southern air is like an invisible molasses. My jeans are drenched, my shirt a different color now. I'm sore from starting to get my body back in shape. I'm a baby. I don't deserve all these gifts.

Almost home, I saw a silver Mercedes-Benz pulled over.

"Excuse me!"

A middle-aged woman with her dark hair done up southern style and donning a deeply red lipstick looked at me somewhere between scared and smiling.

"The Lord told me to turn around," she said. "I saw you. Are you okay? Do you need prayers?"

I looked at her as if she was sent for me. I wondered if this happens often here or it was just me and her and the kids and the fact that I have made a career out of looking this angry.

"I'm sorry?"

"Do you know Jesus Christ?"

I thought about it.

Yes, I do. I know of him. I see him in my mind sometimes, sometimes in my heart. I like who he was. What he represented. He hung out with paupers and prostitutes. He inspired the outcast to feel whole. He was a Jim Jones–type character but he wasn't out to compensate for anything. Basically, he wasn't in it for the power, as far as we know. Oh yeah, he was also the son of God, apparently.

"Yeah, I know him. Thank you." And I walked away.

As I continued to head home I thought about the miracle I had just denied. Why did I not hold her hands and pray with her? What could it have hurt?

How did she know I was in pain?

There was a woman years ago when I was working in the Bahamas who came up to me in a grocery store and said, "You have sad eyes. You have the saddest eyes I have ever seen." Then she simply walked away.

I never forgot that moment.

It's been stuck inside me ever since.

2023

I SHOULD'VE TAKEN EVERYTHING, I thought to myself. Cormac had died just a few days before, and now I was standing in the middle of his house, alone, looking at everything he left behind. I looked at the pool table that we never played on. The bookshelves I would peruse as he was sitting on the far couch in front of the fire, nursing a steak and onions that his son John had cooked up while I asked him what authors he liked best: "I don't know. Ugh. I don't know," he'd respond with great disgust. There were the two grand paintings of one parrot, each to my right. His typewriter that he wrote the last twenty-five or thirty years of books on was at the foot of his bed behind me and to the right, sitting sadly on a carved-out piece of wood to hold it steady on his mattress.

I did ask Cormac to sign my typewriter once a few years ago. A weak moment. A human moment. "Oh, no. Why? If I sign yours then I'll end up having to sign others." I was embarrassed and rightly so. I was putting my connection with him above our friendship. It didn't make any sense. I understand that now. It was an ask that trivialized that friendship. Let collectors pay top dollar for some dirty underwear that might hold the atoms of genius in it. Let them hold it in their hands, bring it up to their faces, rub its magic into their pores. Let them do that.

During one of those days, following that moment I helped him take delusional sips of a glass of Diet Coke the night before he died, I walked into his closet and saw a pair of his boots. I stood there and looked down at them, remembering conversations we had had about Sam Shepard and the fact that Cormac had never read a word of his writing, even though they had been friends. There were also, hanging, the tweed sport jackets he was known to often wear: smart clothes or, probably, just clothes that he could afford at the time, still there. Then the culturally appropriate safe in the closet with, I'm sure, a few rifles and handguns inside. I didn't attempt to open the safe. Most of the rest of the clothing was covered in the plastic they put on dry cleaning after the fact.

I thought of when I walked into the closet of my mother's at the ranch the day after she died. I put her sweater against my face but any remnant of her was long gone. This felt similar. Cormac was gone. I was going to miss him.

Just under a year later there was an auction. His desk was being sold, one that he had made from cherry wood in Tennessee years ago. The desk was starting at fifteen thousand dollars. A feeling came over me. "I should have that desk," I heard myself say. If I had that desk, my writing may improve. Then that infection grew. I pictured myself walking around his house alone. Cormac's place. His home of twenty-five years. His solace, whatever that meant to him. I was vacillating between friend at a loss and scumbag.

He was just a guy. He said to me he didn't even understand why he wrote the way he did: "I don't know why. I just sit down, and it comes, and I type it. Does there have to be a reason? I don't know what it is. I don't care." Simple. There was the work, then there were those responding to the work. That's it. You're a genius and you're a disaster of an artist are close cousins, I've come to realize.

The hollow wanting that passed through me was followed by shame. How dare I be so human, so mediocre. "I should've taken a bunch of shit" is all that feeling was: the tweed coats, the cowboy boots, the knickknacks, paper, books, dirt, the trash. And the shame that followed was because I knew I wasn't doing it to be protective of my friend. It was because I was like everybody else: looking for validity. "This is Cormac's underwear. I rub it in my face. Do you want to rub it in yours? Let's be ordinary together."

It's tough being weak—human—whatever you want to call it. It's embarrassing as all hell.

1976/1995/2021

BIRDS ARE CHIRPING WILDLY OUTSIDE. My little, cramped office window is opened a crack to let some cold air in because the blasting heater blowing right onto my thighs from under the desk won't let up.

We went through my mother's old cookbooks that flank me last night. Kathryn wants to make one of her dishes. There are reams of recipes, all in her writing, and all written on either a restaurant's personal notepads, or napkins, or any scrap of paper she could get her hands on. Every restaurant she'd go into she'd always end up in the kitchen asking a barrage of questions as to how they prepared their dishes differently from how she had, or what new dishes they were making that she could personalize at home (and probably improve on). She'd make herself known. She couldn't help herself. And those old handwritten recipes remind me of our times on the road talking on the CB to wayward truckers who we'd end up meeting at an agreed-on truck stop somewhere along whatever highway we were on. Those eighteen-wheeler Peterbilts, Macks, and Kenworths framed by Christmasy parking lights shimmering against a howling desert wind and in the background those big truckers visible through the large-paned window sitting on stools against the wraparound counter, all their snap button-down dirty white shirts and heavily calloused oil-stained fingers resting on tins of Copenhagen or packs of Pall Mall cigarettes.

All the waitresses in these places were prune-skinned women who had taken care of men like these their whole lives and they smiled a great smile, hoping always to make an extra twenty or thirty cents over what might be just a half a smile back.

And there'd she be, my mom, walking in there, me shuffling at her side, replete with Bruce Lee T-shirt and jeans frayed below my pair of semiworn cowboy boots clacking on the parking lot asphalt; and all the men would look up to her three-hundred-pound voice they had come to know through those CB lines and there she'd be, all 105 pounds of her, rhinestoned and leather fringed: the ready-made blonde raring to go and readily bellowing, "Which one goes by the handle 'Cowboy'?!" and that man would slowly raise a smeared hand, as if someone had just run over it and he'd reply in a voice almost as deep as hers: "Yes, ma'am. That'ad be me." The sea would part as she walked through that truckers' haven, that tilted-mirror pie-displaying oasis.

Cat Lady, they called her. It was because she ran a way station for wild animals in need. It was a fitting handle.

All animal people are crazy. All of them. Dog lovers are not animal people. People who make their tough-as-nails ranch hands go in with a full-grown untrained lion that eventually sinks its teeth into the thigh of one of them and your mom starts laughing so hard she almost can't say "Well, you better get outta there" are animal people, and they're batshit crazy. I grew up with them. I was raised by them, and I understand them, fortunately or not.

Truckers are as close to human animals as you can get. They're feral and act on instinct. Given that, they were the demographic my mother was able to secure because otherwise she was an alien to everybody else. People outside of that trucker social club loved her, but after a while they'd realize they were swimming with a shark: an anomaly, a dare. Everyone wants to swim with a shark every once in a while because it makes them feel as if they're of a chosen, special few who were meant to survive it. They might even want to go back and test it. And so, people would, and they'd leave time and time again, bitten.

But the one thing she could do without any hassle was cook. She'd leave food on people's fence posts at the start of their dirt driveways, and they'd wave at us the next day as she was taking me to school. She'd help start small, local restaurants in the area, then talk about starting her own. Hell, she even filled the fridge with six dishes of dessert the night she died. Three days later, when we had the gathering at the ranch to honor her, that's what everyone ate, her sweet creations, the only sweet she could muster. She moved insides, my mother. Even when she was dead.

So from these strewn scraps of recipe ingredients comes a history and with that chicken scratch history my wife will attempt with our little girls to enliven it once again.

She'll always be somewhere.

She refuses to not be a presence.

The perpetual apparition of Jane.

Dirt

2 sm. instant vanilla
  puddings (Made)
8 oz. cream cheese
1/2 Stick butter
1 cup powdered sugar
8 oz. Cool whip

1 pkg. Oreos

Crush oreos +
Put 1/2 in pot,
then pudding
mixture, then
rest of oreos.

2018

THERE IT WAS AGAIN, THAT SILENCE. He'd walked all day with
his pockets full of syllables and letter shavings that he had gathered over the past couple of days. He'd been thinking a lot and
the thoughts were loud but for now, it was quiet. He'd whittled
away fragments and put them into his pockets to figure out later
when the machine wasn't running so hot. But for now that silence
became him as he stopped along the edge of the cliff overlooking
the sea, took all the jagged would-be sentences out with his hands,
and scattered them on the dusty ground where he crouched. It was
early in the morning inside a foggy marine front, and he could feel
the panting of seagulls as they flew overhead to the north, but he
didn't strain to listen to them.

To the west, the onshore breeze was blowing hard enough to
whip the rabbit ears of his inside-out pockets, but he couldn't feel
those either, nor himself really.

And as he looked down at all those fragmented thoughts, he
kept stopping himself from piecing together a coherent sentence,
from structuring what the architecture of that breeze wanted to,
because it wasn't right, not yet. Nothing was coming together
intuitively. No, he stood there with his head down, focused on
the potpourri. He watched it as if he were standing bedside at his
grandfather's hospice knowing that soon there wouldn't be another

word uttered from his pruned mouth; silence but for these absurd brushstrokes of life shriveling. He reached down, and picked up the grunt or a moan he heard in this memory, and started in again. He felt a cool wind, and with it imagined the smoke of his mother's Kool Kings being sucked out of her driver's-side window. Then he sat down on the dirt and kept shuffling the sounds until came: "The child's laughter shook in him something so violent that he couldn't help but laugh. He put her on his shoulders, her holding intertwined hands across his forehead, and they walked to the ice-cream store for some soft serve—half chocolate, half vanilla—her mouth gnawing at his short hair from above as they walked . . ." It was as far as he could get when he looked up, saw another seagull pass above him, heard the breakwater below, and felt it all; then he went right back into it, slowly, word by infant word.

2023

(Reema)

SHE MADE IT SO SHE COULD TRAVEL, and in traveling she could peek into all that the people did and do, as aligned with her interests. It might have come by the way she grew up. It might have had something to do with her stepfather, Seth.

Regardless, as a little girl she had always been fascinated with why people did what they did, so she made it her business—a photographer, a playwright, a journalist—it didn't matter which, whatever would put her at the forefront of that anthill of humanity.

Eventually she found her way around the world. In Sri Lanka she watched a Russian tattoo being buzzed onto the thick skin of an old man who had almost no room left on his body for more art, and she asked him about the history of his so-visible journal; he told her because she was interested, because she listened intently. She visited a new rehabilitation program started in the Netherlands and spoke to the patients and wondered about the brain and chemistry and what birds do if they get bored, then she checked herself in as an experiment and she learned a great deal about choices and that the word *freedom* can have hiding places too. She ran with a little hustler in Rome and helped pickpocket obese tourists or anybody with a camera strap around their neck and she did an unrelenting sweat with some of the Natives of the Americas in the red hills of New Mexico and saw visions of animals she had never seen before but looked up later and saw actually existed. She ran with devils, and she ran with angels, and most of the time she couldn't tell the differences between the two. The more she traveled, the more she experienced, the more the world came together. Africa had a particular impact on her as she writhed on the ground, parasites attacking her viscera, when small children came to her aid, applying pastes on her forehead, holding their hands on her stomach like you would a casket. She can still feel those little hands on her stomach, which took most of the pain away.

There was surfing in Australia with the wild and whimsical, gray-bearded Barton Lynch and that moment with the shark, then there was the movie set in Wadi Rum, Jordan, when she spent three nights in the glass globe out in the middle of the desert sands and spoke to someone who didn't speak English about the constellation of stars above them and what it meant to the ancients. She learned, and with each experience she knew a little less.

After years of travel, she sat down one day to write a book about who she had met, and all she had learned. With a number two pencil in hand she started to write:

We now see each other with all our foibles, all our scars. There is no hiding anymore. It's a total exposure. Yet the mystery is still there because we are all morphing every day: each decision, each reaction to someone, each necessity and desire manifested on one platform or another. We are exposed to so much and it is overwhelming and inclusive in the same moment. I am grateful for it all: the diarrhea and the diamonds. It's a colorful time, a heated era, and our time here is short and precious. What will define us this year? How will we treat each other? We are responsible for our own destinies. People will shame you in passing, just like they did in school; or, in turn, you may be the shamer, that puffed-up bully who shoulder checks the smaller version of yourself just because it makes you feel

more visible, better equipped. But you too will suffer, because the
law of averages will always find you, be sure of it. So be who you
are but be kind if you can. Honor whatever gifts you may have.
Sing something loudly in the shower or write a nice letter to your
grandmother. We are inside a lucky time really. We are fortunate,
as a species, to have anything at all.

Reema slumped over her words and read them a few times over. She liked what it said, where it came from, but it didn't do justice to all that lived in her; it read more like a letter to a good friend she just needed to unload on than it did a book. She put her pencil down and walked to look out over the Red Sea from the hotel room where she was staying and there she saw a small boat that was just hoisting its sail. She watched it as it filled with the same wind she could feel ruffle the back of her head, making it seem that she had something to do with what would ultimately push that boat out into the sea. She knew she wouldn't write any more, as she couldn't make heads or tails out of the title anyway.

People were kind to her, she thought to herself, and she was kind to them. Everything was shared: a little of this, for a little of that.

2023

THE SEA REMINDS ME OF HER. Years now have passed, and every time I'm away—in the desert, in the mountains—I feel that yearning for the, albeit insane, unpredictability of the sea. She holds my mother after we scattered her ashes into the river that crosses our property there on the Central Coast, ending up, eventually, where it is we all come from: the sea. We wondered among us if her ashes might find their way into the potable water of all the nearby wells and render everyone with the Crazy Jane bullfrogged croak, at least for a day or two: remnants of what just was. It made us laugh. We hoped, in our absurd and needy ways, that we could hear that voice of hers just one last time, even with the assaultive base of it. She was funny. She was unique. She was all the things most have become so deathly afraid of being today: different; not as an affectation, but as a mineral. I see her in my children, the way they accentuate a point or discover awe in what would otherwise seem mundane, but in ways a little less destructive, a little more at peace. My mother at peace, imagine.

Just recently there were several Super 8 reels revealed with her running around as a little girl. To see my mother as a little girl confused me; in my mind she has always been an electric adult. And as I watched those scratchy, faded colors with her smiling as she ran about, I looked to my left and right and there were my little girls doing the same with similar smiles and similar glints of mischief in their eyes. I like it. It moves me knowing that they have inside them what freedom she demanded. It was her lack of grace in that freedom that drove her insane, or at least right to the edge of insanity. I don't see that in my kids.

There is so much to write about. There are so many stories to tell. I guess I'm looking for a deeper sense to it all. That world was *huge*, and the world is now more literal. I haven't decided which I like better.

ACKNOWLEDGMENTS

My unmitigated and immeasurable thanks to . . .

Kimberly Witherspoon: my agent, my guardian angel. You took the pile of broken and burned detritus that was my first compiled fifty pages and you demanded a better, more comprehensive, more honest me. You course corrected hidden agendas I hadn't told anyone about (I still don't understand how you knew), and you always, somehow, found my hand through the phone when I needed something true, and you were as true as though you were actually next to me. Without you there wouldn't be a book, but rather some book-like substance dying in a dark corner of my home. So thank you from the bottom of my heart for being my lighthouse.

My dear, dear pal Anthony Zerbe, for putting on my doorstep the grand works of novelists and poets and prose magicians and painters of language from the moment I met you at twenty years old. For it was you who saw in me something that I could not see in myself back then and I still have trouble seeing clearly today. You saved every postcard I sent and every scrap of paper I ever left behind. You are the greatest friend I have ever had or could ever hope for. You were there with my mother, and you were there with the worst of me, and you always had a smile ready for me to come home to. I would not be filled by all the tickling that literature is if it hadn't been for you. I love you deeply, my friend.

Noah Eaker, you have been my committed editor/partner in refining this dust devil of a book and were right at my side as we navigated its Wild West trajectory. Mostly though, you insisted I keep my voice through every uncertainty, even though your suggestions were always spot on. I cannot thank you enough for taking this on and never once making it feel like it was being pulled away from me. You are a virtuous man and a true artist.

Also, I want to thank assistant editor Edie Astley. Thank you for everything that you put into making this book come to fruition. I have a feeling you might be the first person who read it at Harper-Collins. I might be wrong, but I have a feeling.

Ericka Bonilla, for printing out all those pages, putting the puzzle of emails and calls together, and for having my back when my plate was oozing too full and my mind was mush.

Ethan Coen, I hate you for being so honest. I mean, God, man. You have been that from the very beginning of our friendship, starting almost twenty years ago, and you haven't disappointed once. Your word is golden, which is why you are one of only two friends I gave a ninety-thousand-word draft for opinion and notes to. I sometimes wish I had sent you *War and Peace* and just changed the names and told you I really needed your two cents. Your quiet torture delights me and always will.

Zev Borrow, the other half of this literary Jewish mafia intelligentsia—you have championed this book and its contents forward but never without a deep excitement or an insightful challenge. Like Ethan, your honesty moves me. There are only but a few who give it to me straight, and your insight has always forced me into more clarity. Thank you for always being there.

I don't know how to properly thank my wife, Kathryn. We are inseparable and inevitable, so thanking you feels the lesser expression. Yes, our marriage and partnership in parenting I'd take over my best worst day ever because you are part of the fabric of what